Math
ADVANTAGE

Stretch Your Thinking

ENRICHMENT WORKBOOK

Harcourt Brace & Company

Orlando • Atlanta • Austin • Boston • San Francisco • Chicago • Dallas • New York • Toronto • London

http://www.hbschool.com

CONTENTS

Sums to 10

Color the animals to show ways to make 10.
Write the addition sentence.

1.

_____ + _____ = 10

2.

_____ + _____ = 10

3.

_____ + _____ = 10

4.

_____ + _____ = 10

5.

_____ + _____ = 10

Order Property

Write the sum.
Then write a number sentence to show another way
the addends equal the sum.

1.

$2 + 3 = \underline{5}$

$\underline{3} + \underline{2} = \underline{5}$

2.

$4 + 5 = \underline{\hspace{1cm}}$

$\underline{\hspace{1cm}} + \underline{\hspace{1cm}} = \underline{\hspace{1cm}}$

3.

$6 + 1 = \underline{\hspace{1cm}}$

$\underline{\hspace{1cm}} + \underline{\hspace{1cm}} = \underline{\hspace{1cm}}$

4.

$7 + 2 = \underline{\hspace{1cm}}$

$\underline{\hspace{1cm}} + \underline{\hspace{1cm}} = \underline{\hspace{1cm}}$

5.

$1 + 5 = \underline{\hspace{1cm}}$

$\underline{\hspace{1cm}} + \underline{\hspace{1cm}} = \underline{\hspace{1cm}}$

6.

$2 + 5 = \underline{\hspace{1cm}}$

$\underline{\hspace{1cm}} + \underline{\hspace{1cm}} = \underline{\hspace{1cm}}$

7.

$1 + 4 = \underline{\hspace{1cm}}$

$\underline{\hspace{1cm}} + \underline{\hspace{1cm}} = \underline{\hspace{1cm}}$

8.

$8 + 2 = \underline{\hspace{1cm}}$

$\underline{\hspace{1cm}} + \underline{\hspace{1cm}} = \underline{\hspace{1cm}}$

9.

$7 + 3 = \underline{\hspace{1cm}}$

$\underline{\hspace{1cm}} + \underline{\hspace{1cm}} = \underline{\hspace{1cm}}$

10.

$9 + 1 = \underline{\hspace{1cm}}$

$\underline{\hspace{1cm}} + \underline{\hspace{1cm}} = \underline{\hspace{1cm}}$

Zero Property

Fill in the missing addends.

1. $2 + \underline{0} = 2$ $\underline{0} + 2 = 2$

2. $\underline{\quad} + 0 = 6$ $0 + \underline{\quad} = 6$

3. $0 + \underline{\quad} = 9$ $9 + \underline{\quad} = 9$

4. $0 + \underline{\quad} = 3$ $3 + \underline{\quad} = 3$

5. $\underline{\quad} + 4 = 4$ $\underline{\quad} + 0 = 4$

6. $\underline{\quad} + 7 = 7$ $\underline{\quad} + 0 = 7$

7. $1 + \underline{\quad} = 1$ $\underline{\quad} + 0 = 1$

8. $\underline{\quad} + 0 = 5$ $\underline{\quad} + 5 = 5$

Counting On

Fill in the numbers.

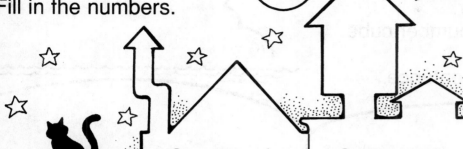

		Count on 1.	Count on 2.	Count on 3.
1.	7	$7 + 1 = 8$	$7 + 2 = 9$	$7 + 3 = 10$
2.	3	__ + __ = __	__ + __ = __	__ + __ = __
3.	5	__ + __ = __	__ + __ = __	__ + __ = __
4.	6	__ + __ = __	__ + __ = __	__ + __ = __
5.	4	__ + __ = __	__ + __ = __	__ + __ = __
6.	2	__ + __ = __	__ + __ = __	__ + __ = __
7.	1	__ + __ = __	__ + __ = __	__ + __ = __
8.	7	__ + __ = __	__ + __ = __	__ + __ = __

Addition Practice

Work with a partner.
Each of you roll a number cube.
Add the 2 numbers.
Write the number sentence.

1. ____ ◯ ____ = ____

2. ____ ◯ ____ = ____

3. ____ ◯ ____ = ____

4. ____ ◯ ____ = ____

5. ____ ◯ ____ = ____

6. ____ ◯ ____ = ____

7. ____ ◯ ____ = ____

8. ____ ◯ ____ = ____

Differences Through 10

Subtract. Find the difference in the box.
Color the kite part to match.

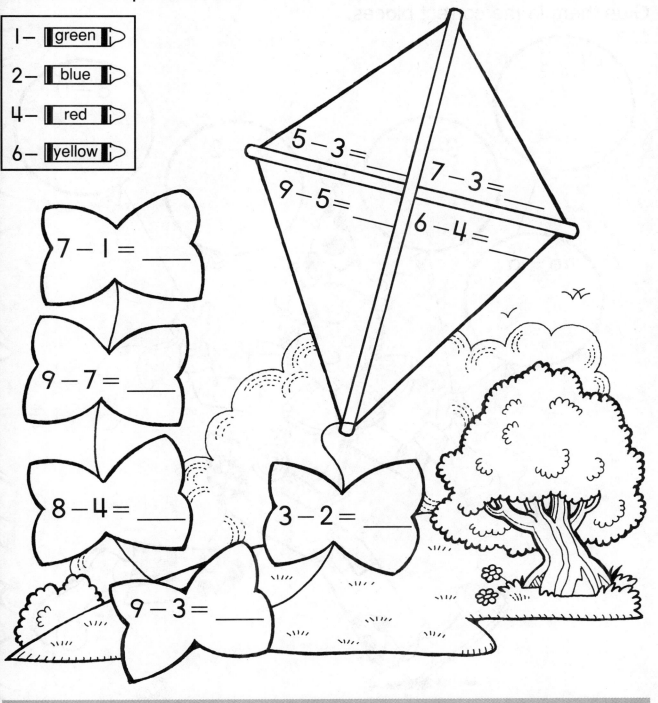

1 – green
2 – blue
4 – red
6 – yellow

5 – 3 = ___

7 – 3 = ___

9 – 5 = ___

6 – 4 = ___

7 – 1 = ___

9 – 7 = ___

8 – 4 = ___

3 – 2 = ___

9 – 3 = ___

STRETCH YOUR THINKING   E9

Subtracting All or Zero

Subtract.
Cut out the squares at the bottom.
Glue them in the correct places.

4 − 4

8 − 0

3 − 0

2 − 2

6 − 6

| 0 | 8 | 0 | 3 | 0 |

Using Subtraction to Compare

Write the numbers under the flowers.
Subtract to find how many more.

1.

__6__ 🌷 – __4__ 🌼 = __2__   __2__ more 🌷

2.

____ 🌷 – ____ 🌹 = ____   ____ more 🌷

3.

____ 🌸 – ____ 🌻 = ____   ____ more 🌸

4.

____ 🌼 – ____ 🌹 = ____   ____ more 🌼

Counting Back

Think of the number. Count back.
Write the number.

	Think.	Count back.	
1.	7	3	_4_
2.	4	2	___
3.	6	1	___
4.	5	2	___
5.	9	3	___
6.	8	4	___

Problem Solving • Make a Model

Work with a partner. Think of the problem-solving steps.
What is missing? Use counters to make a model.
Write what you need to know to solve each problem.

1. There are 16 red flowers in the garden.
   There are yellow flowers, too.
   How many flowers are there in all?

   I need to know _____

   _____

   _____

2. Jenny has 6 red shirts.
   She has green shirts, too.
   How many shirts does she have?

   I need to know _____

   _____

   _____

3. Garrett has 6 grapes.
   He ate some of them.
   How many grapes does he have left?

   I need to know _____

   _____

   _____

Doubles Stories

Use counters. Complete the problems.

1. Kay sees 6 blue birds and the same number of red birds. How many birds does she see in all?

   __12__ birds

2. Ralph sees 5 butterflies. Then 5 more join them. How many butterflies does Ralph see in all?

   _____ butterflies

3. Don sees a group of birds. Then 8 more birds join the group. He sees 16 birds in all. How many birds did he see in the first group?

   _____ birds

4. Maria sees 9 frogs. Then more frogs join them. She sees 18 frogs in all. How many more frogs joined the group?

   _____ frogs

5. John sees 4 bugs. Faye sees twice as many bugs as John. How many bugs did they see in all?

   _____ bugs

More Doubles

Beth collected shells at the beach.
The first day she collected 1 shell.
Each day after that, she collected **double**
the number she collected the day before, **plus** 1.
Color in the chart to show how many shells
she collected.

Number of Shells Collected

	1	2	3	4	5	6	7	8	9	10	11	12	13	14	15	16
Day 1	▨															
Day 2	▨	▨	▨													
Day 3																
Day 4																

How many shells did Beth collect on Day 4? _____ shells

Birds Everywhere!

Complete each table.
Color the birds to check.

1. There are 13 birds.
   9 birds are yellow.
   How many are **not** yellow?

Birds in All	Yellow	Not Yellow
13	9	

2. There are 15 birds.
   9 birds are blue.
   How many are **not** blue?

Birds in All	Blue	Not Blue

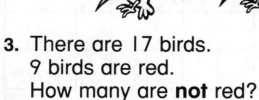

3. There are 17 birds.
   9 birds are red.
   How many are **not** red?

Birds in All	Red	Not Red

Make a Ten

Write the sum. Use the code to solve the word puzzle.

1. $\begin{array}{r} 8 \\ + 3 \\ \hline 11 \end{array}$

2. $\begin{array}{r} 7 \\ + 5 \\ \hline \end{array}$

3. $\begin{array}{r} 6 \\ + 7 \\ \hline \end{array}$

4. $\begin{array}{r} 9 \\ + 8 \\ \hline \end{array}$

5. $\begin{array}{r} 5 \\ + 5 \\ \hline \end{array}$

6. $\begin{array}{r} 5 \\ + 9 \\ \hline \end{array}$

7. $\begin{array}{r} 8 \\ + 8 \\ \hline \end{array}$

8. $\begin{array}{r} 9 \\ + 6 \\ \hline \end{array}$

9. $\begin{array}{r} 3 \\ + 4 \\ \hline \end{array}$

10. $\begin{array}{r} 8 \\ + 5 \\ \hline \end{array}$

11. $\begin{array}{r} 6 \\ + 3 \\ \hline \end{array}$

12. $\begin{array}{r} 7 \\ + 4 \\ \hline \end{array}$

13. $\begin{array}{r} 4 \\ + 4 \\ \hline \end{array}$

14. $\begin{array}{r} 4 \\ + 2 \\ \hline \end{array}$

6	7	8	9	10	11	12	13	14	15	16	17
!	N	E	O	I	M	A	T	S	U	F	H

1.	2.	3.	4.		5.	6.		7.	8.	9.
M	A	T								

10.	11.		12.	13.	14.

Adding Three Addends

Use three number cubes.
Work with a friend.
Roll to make addends.
Write the sum.

	Roll 1	Roll 2	Roll 3	Total
1.				
2.				
3.				
4.				
5.				
6.				
7.				
8.				
9.				
10.				

Relating Addition and Subtraction

Write the addition or subtraction sentence. Solve.

1. Li had 8 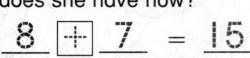.

She won 7 more.

How many

does she have now?

__8__ ⊞ __7__ = __15__

Brad had 15 .

He gave away 7.

How many

does he have left?

____ ☐ ____ = ____

---

2. Marco had 9 .

He found 9 more.

How many

does Marco have now?

____ ☐ ____ = ____

Maria had 18 .

She gave 9 to her

friends. How many

does Maria have now?

____ ☐ ____ = ____

---

3. Tamika had 9 .

Then she got 5 more.

How many

does she have in all?

____ ☐ ____ = ____

Gino had 14 .

He gave 5 away. How many

does he have left?

____ ☐ ____ = ____

---

4. Ashley saw 5 big

and 6 little .

How many

did she see in all?

____ ☐ ____ = ____

Tom saw 11 in a

little car. Then 6 jumped out.

How many were left

in the car?

____ ☐ ____ = ____

Subtracting on a Number Line

What is at Story Land Park?
Subtract on the number line to find out.
Write the letter of each difference.

```
0  1  2  3  4  5  6  7  8  9  10 11 12 13 14 15 16 17 18 19
A  B  C  D  E  F  G  H  I  J  K  L  M  N  O  P  Q  R  S  T
```

1. $\dfrac{C}{4-2}$ $\dfrac{}{8-8}$ $\dfrac{}{19-0}$

2. $\dfrac{}{10-5}$ $\dfrac{}{11-3}$ $\dfrac{}{4-1}$ $\dfrac{}{7-4}$ $\dfrac{}{12-1}$ $\dfrac{}{9-5}$

3. $\dfrac{}{5-2}$ $\dfrac{}{17-3}$ $\dfrac{}{12-6}$

4. $\dfrac{}{15-3}$ $\dfrac{}{18-4}$ $\dfrac{}{16-2}$ $\dfrac{}{18-5}$

5. $\dfrac{}{8-5}$ $\dfrac{}{14-6}$ $\dfrac{}{19-1}$ $\dfrac{}{10-3}$

Fact Families

Cut out the number cards. Make a group
with each row of cards. Choose one card from
each group to make the addends. Then write
the numbers in the fact family in the boxes.

1.

_____ + _____ = _____   _____ − _____ = _____

_____ + _____ = _____   _____ − _____ = _____

2.

_____ + _____ = _____   _____ − _____ = _____

_____ + _____ = _____   _____ − _____ = _____

3.

_____ + _____ = _____   _____ − _____ = _____

_____ + _____ = _____   _____ − _____ = _____

1	2	3	4	5	6	7	8	9	10

1	2	3	4	5	6	7	8	9	10

Missing Addends

Find the missing addend.
Then use the crayon for that number to color the picture.

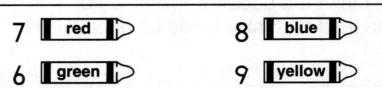

7 red

8 blue

6 green

9 yellow

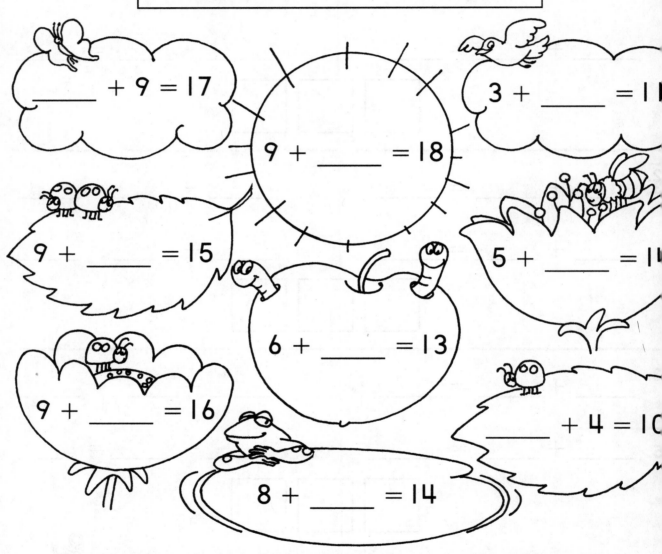

_____ + 9 = 17

9 + _____ = 18

3 + _____ = 1

9 + _____ = 15

5 + _____ = 1

6 + _____ = 13

9 + _____ = 16

_____ + 4 = 10

8 + _____ = 14

Mystery Numbers!

Solve.

1. Two numbers are added.
The sum is 16.
The first number is 7.
What is the other number?

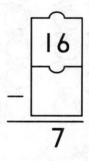

7
+ 9

16

2. Two numbers are added.
The sum is 14.
The first number is 8.
What is the other number?

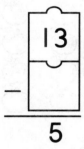

8
+

14

3. A number is subtracted from 16. The difference is 7.
What is the other number?

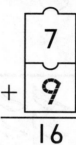

16
−

7

4. A number is subtracted from 13. The difference is 5.
What is the other number?

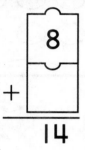

13
−

5

5. One number is subtracted from another. The subtracted number is 4.
The difference is 8.
What is the other number?

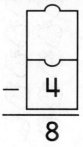

− 4

8

6. One number is subtracted from another. The subtracted number is 6.
The difference is 9.
What is the other number?

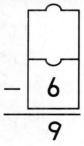

− 6

9

Name _____

Fruit by the Numbers

Which is greater?
Circle the number or the picture.

1.

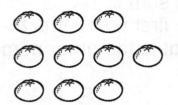   or **(70)**

2.

or **20**

3.

or **40**

4.

   or **50**

5.

   or **80**

Riddle Me This

Read a riddle to a friend.
Have your friend solve it. Take turns.

1. I am thinking of a number.
It is greater than 5 tens
and 2 ones. It is less than 5
tens and 4 ones.
What is the number?

<u>53</u>

2. I am thinking of a number.
It is greater than 3 tens
and 3 ones. It is less than
3 tens and 5 ones.
What is the number?

_____

3. I am thinking of two numbers.
They are both greater than
I ten and 4 ones. They are
both less than I ten and 7 ones.
What are the numbers?

_____ _____

4. I am thinking of two numbers.
They are both greater than 2
tens and 5 ones. They are both
less than 2 tens and 8 ones.
What are the numbers?

_____ _____

5. I am thinking of two numbers.
They are both greater than 3
tens and 5 ones. They are both
less than 3 tens and 8 ones.
What are the numbers?

_____ _____

6. I am thinking of two numbers.
They are both greater than 2
tens and 2 ones. They are both
less than 2 tens and 5 ones.
What are the numbers?

_____ _____

Puzzle Time

Solve the problem. Then write the answer
as tens and ones in the puzzle.

1. | 5 | t | e | n | s | | 9 | o | n | e | s |

2. | | t | e | n | s | | | o | n | e | s |

Across

1. Karen had 53 stars.
Joe gave her 6 more.
How many stars
does she have in all? _____

2. John has 42 baseball
cards. Sergio has 3 more
than John. How many
cards does Sergio
have? _____

Down

1. Sam had 75 stickers.
He gave 5 away.
How many stickers
does he have left? _____

2. Wendy has 63 stamps.
She put 10 on a page.
How many stamps
does she have left? _____

Numbers! Numbers!

Write the number as tens and ones.

1. 82 = __80__ + __2__

2. 19 = _____ + _____

3. 24 = _____ + _____

4. 57 = _____ + _____

5. 68 = _____ + _____

6. 46 = _____ + _____

7. 33 = _____ + _____

8. 93 = _____ + _____

9. 41 = _____ + _____

10. 75 = _____ + _____

Add tens and ones. Write the sum.

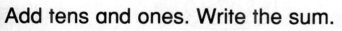

11. 30 + 5 = _____

12. 40 + 4 = _____

13. 50 + 9 = _____

14. 90 + 8 = _____

15. 60 + 2 = _____

16. 70 + 6 = _____

17. 20 + 3 = _____

18. 30 + 1 = _____

19. 80 + 7 = _____

20. 50 + 5 = _____

STRETCH YOUR THINKING   E27

Exploring Estimation

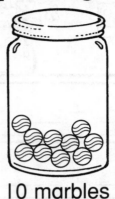
10 marbles

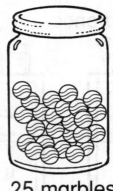
25 marbles

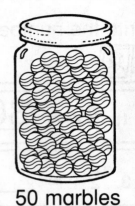
50 marbles

Look at each group of marbles.
Use these groups to help you estimate.

1.

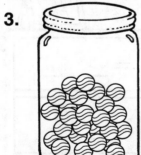

about _____
marbles

2.

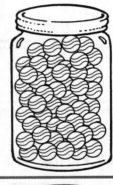

about _____
marbles

3.

about _____
marbles

4.

about _____
marbles

5.

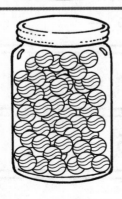

about _____
marbles

6.

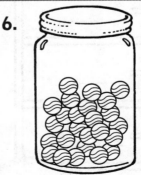

about _____
marbles

Number Patterns

Count by fours. Circle the numbers.

1	2	3	(4)	5	6	7	8	9	10
11	12	13	14	15	16	17	18	19	20
21	22	23	24	25	26	27	28	29	30
31	32	33	34	35	36	37	38	39	40
41	42	43	44	45	46	47	48	49	50
51	52	53	54	55	56	57	58	59	60
61	62	63	64	65	66	67	68	69	70
71	72	73	74	75	76	77	78	79	80
81	82	83	84	85	86	87	88	89	90
91	92	93	94	95	96	97	98	99	100

The numbers with circles end with 0, 2, 4, _____, or _____.

They never end with 1, 3, _____, _____, or _____.

Skip-Counting by Twos and Threes

Follow the paths to the cabin.
Count by twos and by threes.
Write the numbers.

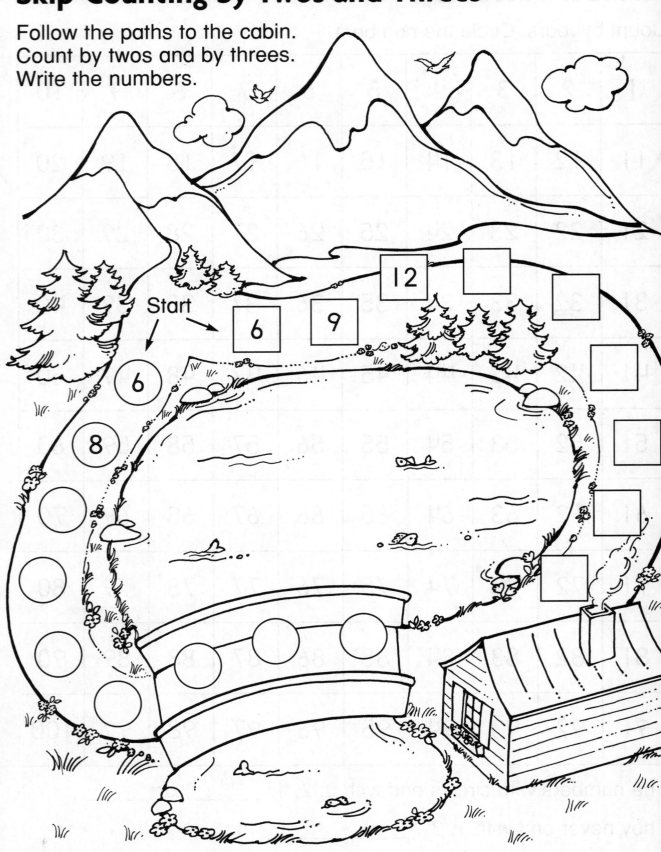

Start

6

9

12

6

8

Even and Odd Numbers

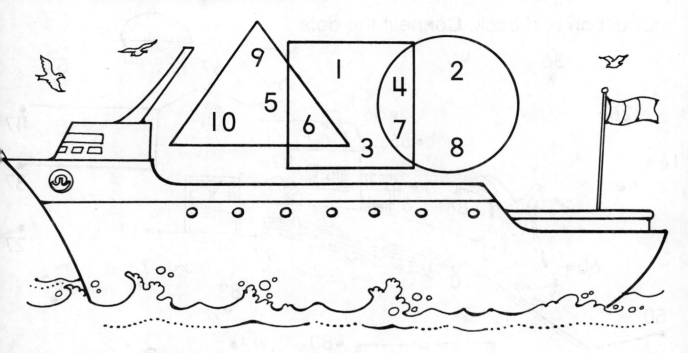

Use the clues to answer the riddle.
Then circle **even** or **odd**.

1. This number is inside the square. It is also inside the triangle. What number is it?

_____

even   odd

2. This number is inside only the circle. The number is less than 5. What number is it?

_____

even   odd

3. This number is inside the triangle. The number is greater than 9. What number is it?

_____

even   odd

4. This number is inside the square. It is also inside the circle. The number is greater than 6. What number is it?

_____

even   odd

Counting On and Back by Tens

Count on and back. Connect the dots.

36   46   67   57

26   56   77   47

16   66

6   87   37

86   76   17

60   70   97   73   27

                  83   63

50   93

                  80   5

                  103   33   43

40

30   20   90   71

                        61

                        51

                  41   21   11
                        31   1

Problem Solving • Look for a Pattern

Complete the table.

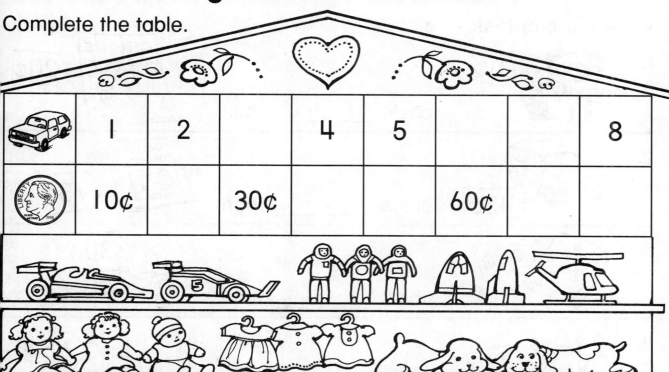

	1	2		4	5			8
	10¢		30¢			60¢		

Use the table to answer the questions.

1. Travis wants to buy 5 toy cars. How much money does he need?

_____ ¢

2. Whitney wants to buy 4 toy cars. How much money does she need?

_____ ¢

3. Jessica wants to buy 7 toy cars. How much money does she need?

_____ ¢

4. Bradley has 50¢. How many toy cars can he buy?

_____ toy cars

5. Terry wants to buy 1 toy car. How much money does he need?

_____ ¢

6. Jade has 80¢. How many toy cars can she buy?

_____ toy cars

Comparing Numbers

Write **more** or **less**.

1.

costs <u>more</u> than

2.

costs _____ than

3.

costs _____ than

4.

costs _____ than

5.

costs _____ than

Write how much **more** or **less**.

6.

costs <u>30</u> ¢ <u>less</u> than

7.

costs ____ ¢ _____ than

8.

costs ____ ¢ _____ than

Greater Than and Less Than

Write >, <, or = to make a true sentence.

I.

7 + 6 $<$ 14

2.

8 + 8 $\bigcirc$ 16

3.

12 + 13 $\bigcirc$ 19

4.

6 + 9 $\bigcirc$ 12

5.

4 + 9 $\bigcirc$ 8

6.

11 + 9 $\bigcirc$ 21

7.

7 + 8 $\bigcirc$ 15

8.

8 + 4 $\bigcirc$ 10

9.

14 − 5 $\bigcirc$ 8

10.

17 − 8 $\bigcirc$ 12

11.

15 − 7 $\bigcirc$ 5

12.

17 − 9 $\bigcirc$ 8

13.

34 − 10 $\bigcirc$ 22

14.

25 − 14 $\bigcirc$ 19

15.

27 + 13 $\bigcirc$ 40

16.

66 − 33 $\bigcirc$ 33

Ordering Numbers: After, Before, Between

Read the riddle. Write the answer.

1. I am the number that comes before 29 and after 27. What number am I?

<u>28</u>

2. I am the number that comes between 45 and 47. What number am I?

_____

3. I am the number that comes before 38 and after 36. What number am I?

_____

4. I am the number that comes between 78 and 80. What number am I?

_____

5. I am the number that comes between 66 and 68. What number am I?

_____

6. I am the number that comes before 55 and after 53. What number am I?

_____

7. These numbers come after 91 and before 95. What numbers are they?

_____ , _____ , _____

8. These numbers come between 40 and 44. What numbers are they?

_____ , _____ , _____

Ordinal Numbers

A	B	C	D	E	F	G	H	I	J-K
1	2	3	4	5	6	7	8	9	10

L	M	N	O	P	Q-R	S	T	U-V	WXYZ
11	12	13	14	15	16	17	18	19	20

In which book could you read about each animal?
Circle the correct answer.

1.	rabbits	first	ninth	sixteenth
2.	frogs	second	sixth	tenth
3.	turtles	fourth	eleventh	eighteenth
4.	zebras	fifteenth	twelfth	twentieth
5.	kangaroos	tenth	eighth	thirteenth
6.	cats	seventh	third	eleventh

Using a Number Line to Estimate

40 41 42 43 44 45 46 47 48 49 **50** 51 52 53 54 55 56 57 58 59 **60**

I. Start at 40.
Go forward 5 spaces.
Go back 3 spaces.
Write the number. ___42___

Is the number closer
to 40 or 50? ___40___

2. Start at 60.
Go back 11 spaces.
Go forward 8 spaces.
Write the number. _____

Is the number closer
to 50 or 60? _____

3. Start at 50.
Go forward 5 spaces.
Go back 7 spaces.
Write the number. _____

Is the number closer
to 40 or 50? _____

4. Start at 45.
Go forward 4 spaces.
Go back 6 spaces.
Write the number. _____

Is the number closer
to 40 or 50? _____

5. Start at 55.
Go back 9 spaces.
Go forward 7 spaces.
Write the number. _____

Is the number closer
to 50 or 60? _____

6. Start at 52.
Go back 6 spaces.
Go forward 2 spaces.
Write the number. _____

Is the number closer
to 50 or 60? _____

Pennies, Nickels, and Dimes

Work with a friend.
Choose who will be A and who will be B.
Who has the greater amount in each row? Circle it.
If you both have the same amount, work together
to color all the coins.

A	B

1.

2.

3.

4.

5.

Nickels, Dimes, Quarters

Write the total amount for each group.
Color the group of coins that is
worth more than a quarter.

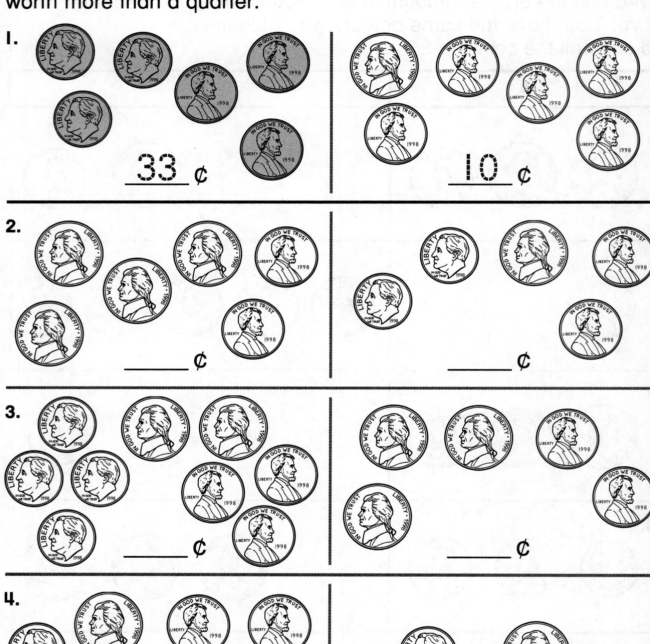

1. _33_ ¢   _10_ ¢

2. _____ ¢   _____ ¢

3. _____ ¢   _____ ¢

4.

_____ ¢

_____ ¢

Counting Collections

Circle the fewest coins that show the amount.

1.

2.

3.

4.

Counting Half-Dollars

Ann can use different numbers of coins
to make the same
amount of money.
Can you?

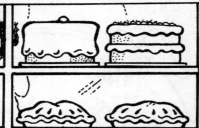

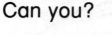

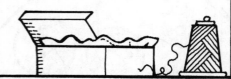

1. Ann buys a muffin that costs 55¢. She uses 3 coins.
Write how many of each coin.

_____   _____   _____   _____   _____

2. Make 55¢ with 2 coins.
Write how many of each coin.

_____   _____   _____   _____   _____

3. Make 55¢ with 5 coins.
Write how many of each coin.

_____   _____   _____   _____   _____

Problem Solving • Act It Out

Marco has   .

Color what he could buy.
He cannot spend more than he has.

Combinations of Coins

Circle the coins you need.

1.

Circle two coins that make 50¢.

2.

Circle four coins that make 50¢.

3.

Circle six coins that make 50¢.

4.

Circle seven coins that make 50¢.

Equal Amounts Using Fewest Coins

Solve. Draw the coins.
Write the value on each coin.

1. Ivan has 43¢.
   He has 9 coins.
   What coins does he have?

 = 43¢

2. Brittany has 43¢.
   She has 6 coins.
   What coins does she have?

= 43¢

3. Jacob has 65¢.
   He has 5 coins.
   What coins does he have?

= 65¢

4. Whitney has 65¢.
   She has 3 coins.
   What coins does she have?

= 65¢

Comparing Amounts to Prices

Solve. Write the amounts.
Circle what the person can buy.

1. Drew has 4 dimes
   and 3 nickels.
   How much money
   does he have?

   _____ ¢

2. Maria has 2 quarters,
   I dime, 2 nickels, and
   I penny. How much
   money does she have?

   _____ ¢

3. Sue has 3 quarters,
   I dime, and I nickel.
   How much money does
   she have?

   _____ ¢

4. Jamila has 2 quarters,
   2 dimes, and 3 pennies.
   How much money does
   she have?

   _____ ¢

Making Change

Use punch-out coins. Use the fewest coins to show the change.
Trace the coins and write the value on each one.
Then write the amount of change in all.

	Price	Pay	Change
1.	60¢	75¢	(5¢) (10¢) ___15___ ¢ change
2.	17¢	50¢	_____ ¢ change
3.	11¢	50¢	_____ ¢ change
4.	51¢	75¢	_____ ¢ change

Coins in the Bank

Solve the problem. Draw the missing coin in the bank.
Write the value on the coin you draw.

1. Mark has 3 dimes and 1 nickel. What coin does he need to buy an eraser that costs 40¢?

2. Amy has 1 quarter and 3 pennies. What coin does she need to buy a pencil that costs 29¢?

3. Olga has 4 dimes. What coin does she need to buy note paper that costs 50¢?

4. Douglas has 2 quarters and 2 nickels. What coin does he need to buy a box of markers that costs 70¢?

5. Brett has 2 dimes and 3 nickels. What coin does he need to buy a pair of scissors that costs 40¢?

6. Akiko has 1 quarter, 2 dimes, and 1 nickel. What coin does she need to buy a notebook that costs 75¢?

Hour and Half-Hour

Read the story to a friend.
Have your friend circle the clock that shows
what time it might happen. Take turns.

1. Marco was dreaming about
his dog. Then his alarm clock
went off.

2. Marco got ready for school.
He walked to school with
his brother.

3. Marco's class watched a play.
After the play, Marco ate lunch.

4. Later, Marco wrote a story
about a robot. Soon it was
time to go home.

5. Marco told his sister about
his story. Then he went
to bed.

Telling Time to 5 Minutes

Draw a line to the clock that comes next.

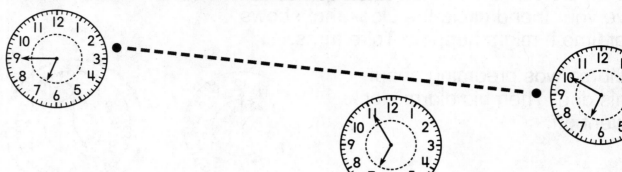

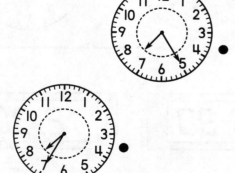

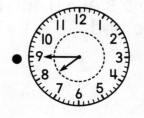

Telling Time to 15 Minutes

Draw the hour hand and the minute hand
to show the time 15 minutes later.

1.

2.

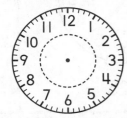

3.

4.

5.

6.

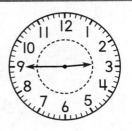
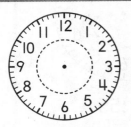

Practice Telling Time

Draw the hour hand and the minute hand to show the time.

1.

1:15

2.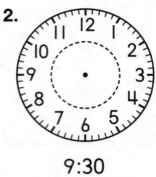

9:30

3.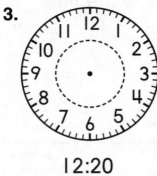

12:20

4.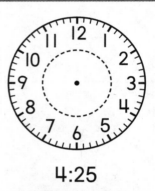

4:25

5.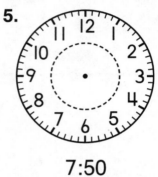

7:50

6.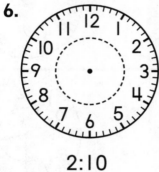

2:10

7.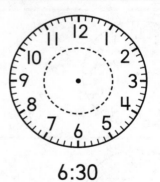

6:30

8.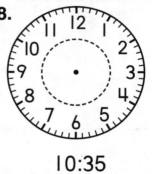

10:35

9.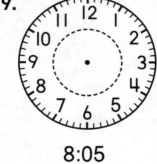

8:05

10.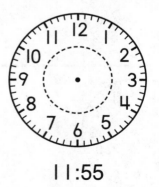

11:55

11.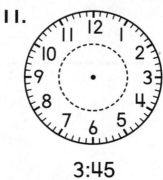

3:45

12.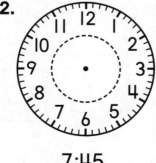

7:45

Elapsed Time

Solve. Write the answer.

1. It is now 8:30.
The mall will close in
30 minutes. What time
will the mall close?

   <u>9:00</u>

2. The race begins at 10:00.
It will end in 1 hour.
What time will the race end?

   _____

3. The play starts at 2:30.
It will end in 2 hours.
What time will the play end?

   _____

4. It is now 3:45.
We will be at Grandpa's
house in 30 minutes.
What time will we be at
his house?

   _____

5. The game ended at 4:00.
It had taken 1 hour.
What time did the game
begin?

   _____

6. The baby woke up at 3:00.
He had slept for 1 hour.
What time did he go to sleep?

   _____

7. The test starts at 1:00.
It will end in 30 minutes.
What time will the test end?

   _____

8. The zoo trip ended at 5:30.
It had lasted 2 hours.
What time did the zoo
trip start?

   _____

Name _____

Reading a Calendar

August

Sunday	Monday	Tuesday	Wednesday	Thursday	Friday	Saturday
					1 Billy	2
3	4	5 Mike	6	7	8	9
10	11	12	13	14	15	16
17	18	19	20	21 Mila	22	23 Todd
24 Julio	25	26	27 Laura	28	29	30
31						

Use the calendar to answer the questions.

1. Who has a birthday on a Wednesday? _____

2. Who has a birthday the same week as Mila? _____

3. Who has a birthday on August 24? _____

4. How many days are between Billy's and
   Mike's birthdays? _____

5. Who has the last birthday in August? _____

Name _____

sing a Calendar

January
S M T W T F S
1 2 3 4
5 6 7 8 9 10 11
12 13 14 15 16 17 18
19 20 21 22 23 24 25
26 27 28 29 30 31

February
S M T W T F S
1
2 3 4 5 6 7 8
9 10 11 (12) 13 14 15
16 17 18 19 20 21 22
23 24 25 26 27 28

March
S M T W T F S
1
2 3 4 5 6 7 8
9 10 11 12 13 14 15
16 17 18 19 20 21 22
23/30 24/31 25 26 27 28 29

April
S M T W T F S
1 2 3 4 5
6 7 8 9 10 11 12
13 14 15 16 17 18 19
20 21 22 23 24 25 26
27 28 29 30

May
S M T W T F S
1 2 3
4 5 6 7 8 9 10
11 12 13 14 15 16 17
18 19 20 21 22 23 24
25 26 27 28 29 30 31

June
S M T W T F S
1 2 3 4 5 6 7
8 9 10 11 12 13 14
15 16 17 18 19 20 21
22 23 24 25 26 27 28
29 30

July
S M T W T F S
1 2 3 4 5
6 7 8 9 10 11 12
13 14 15 16 17 18 19
20 21 22 23 24 25 26
27 28 29 30 31

August
S M T W T F S
1 2
3 4 5 6 7 8 9
10 11 12 13 14 15 16
17 18 19 20 21 22 23
24/31 25 26 27 28 29 30

September
S M T W T F S
1 2 3 4 5 6
7 8 9 10 11 12 13
14 15 16 17 18 19 20
21 22 23 24 25 26 27
28 29 30

October
S M T W T F S
1 2 3 4
5 6 7 8 9 10 11
12 13 14 15 16 17 18
19 20 21 22 23 24 25
26 27 28 29 30 31

November
S M T W T F S
1
2 3 4 5 6 7 8
9 10 11 12 13 14 15
16 17 18 19 20 21 22
23/30 24 25 26 27 28 29

December
S M T W T F S
1 2 3 4 5 6
7 8 9 10 11 12 13
14 15 16 17 18 19 20
21 22 23 24 25 26 27
28 29 30 31

Circle these special dates on the calendar.

1. Lincoln's birthday, February 12.

2. April Fool's Day, April 1.

3. New Year's Day, January 1.

4. Thanksgiving Day, November 27.

5. Earth Day, April 22.

6. Martin Luther King Day, January 20.

7. Flag Day, June 14.

8. Columbus Day, October 12.

Early or Late

Read the story.
Read the question.
Circle the answer.

Kara's Busy Day
Kara has to walk the dog at 1:30. She wants to meet Beth at the park at 2:15. Kara needs to be home at 4:00.

1. Kara walked her dog late.
What time did Kara walk her dog?

1:20

1:35

2. Kara arrived at the park early.
What time did Kara arrive at the park?

2:30

2:00

3. Kara arrived home early.
What time did Kara arrive home?

3:30

4:15

4. How many minutes early did Kara get home?

30 minutes

5 minutes

5. Which clock shows what time Kara got home?

Name _____

Sequencing Events

Juan and his mother are cooking dinner.
Draw a picture to show what will happen after
Juan sets the table.

What might happen next?

Reading a Schedule

You are planning what to do after school today.
Make your schedule.

play outside
one hour

eat a snack
half-hour

do homework
one hour

watch TV
half-hour

I. Show the times you start and finish each activity.

2. Circle blue what you like to do best.

Time	Activity
3:30–	

Regrouping Ones as Tens

Circle three ways to name the same number.

1. (9 + 6)   (1 ten 5 ones)   (15 ones)   9 ones

2. 1 ten 7 ones   9 + 8   2 tens   17 ones

3. 18 ones   1 ten 8 ones   9 + 9   1 ten

4. 3 tens 1 one   1 ten 3 ones   7 + 6   13 ones

5. 1 ten 5 ones   8 + 7   15 ones   15 tens

6. 9 + 5   14 ones   1 ten 4 ones   41 ones

7. 13 ones   8 + 5   11 ones   1 ten 3 ones

8. 1 ten 6 ones   16 ones   8 + 8   8 ones

9. 14 ones   8 + 6   4 tens   1 ten 4 ones

10. 21 ones   1 ten 2 ones   7 + 5   12 ones

Modeling One-Digit and Two-Digit Addition

Add the ones.
Think: Can I make a ten?
Circle the better estimate.

1.

$$\begin{array}{r} 16 \\ + 6 \\ \hline \end{array}$$

(greater than 20)

less than 20

$$\begin{array}{r} 14 \\ + 4 \\ \hline \end{array}$$

greater than 20

less than 20

$$\begin{array}{r} 17 \\ + 5 \\ \hline \end{array}$$

greater than 20

less than 20

2.

$$\begin{array}{r} 26 \\ + 3 \\ \hline \end{array}$$

greater than 30

less than 30

$$\begin{array}{r} 27 \\ + 9 \\ \hline \end{array}$$

greater than 30

less than 30

$$\begin{array}{r} 28 \\ + 8 \\ \hline \end{array}$$

greater than 30

less than 30

3.

$$\begin{array}{r} 37 \\ + 5 \\ \hline \end{array}$$

greater than 40

less than 40

$$\begin{array}{r} 32 \\ + 6 \\ \hline \end{array}$$

greater than 40

less than 40

$$\begin{array}{r} 36 \\ + 7 \\ \hline \end{array}$$

greater than 40

less than 40

4.

$$\begin{array}{r} 45 \\ + 6 \\ \hline \end{array}$$

greater than 50

less than 50

$$\begin{array}{r} 44 \\ + 5 \\ \hline \end{array}$$

greater than 50

less than 50

$$\begin{array}{r} 59 \\ + 8 \\ \hline \end{array}$$

greater than 60

less than 60

Modeling Two-Digit Addition

Use Workmat 3 and base-ten blocks.

1. There are 17 boys skating. Then 16 girls join them. There are _____ children in all skating.	
2. There are 19 robins in the maple tree. Then 18 wrens join them. There are _____ birds in all in the maple tree.	
3. I have 18 pennies. I save 23 more. Now I have _____ pennies.	
4. Marcy's mom baked 24 sugar cookies. Then she baked 12 lemon cookies. She baked _____ cookies in all.	
5. Len counts 29 oak trees in the park. Then he counts 19 elm trees. He counts _____ trees in the park.	

Recording Two-Digit Addition

Read the riddle.
Use base-ten blocks to solve.
Write the answer to the riddle.

1. Two numbers are added.
The sum is 35.
One number is 24.
What is the other number?

$$24 + 11 = 35$$

$$\underline{11}$$

2. Two numbers are added.
The sum is 24.
One number is 12.
What is the other number?

_____

3. Two numbers are added.
The sum is 33.
One number is 18.
What is the other number?

_____

4. Two numbers are added.
The sum is 27.
One number is 11.
What is the other number?

_____

5. Two numbers are added.
The sum is 18.
One number is 7.
What is the other number?

_____

6. Two numbers are added.
The sum is 32.
One number is 16.
What is the other number?

_____

Problem Solving • Make a Model

Circle the correct answer. Use base-ten blocks to find the sums.

1. There are 18 monkeys
   in the zoo.
   There are 15 snakes
   in the zoo.
   How many monkeys and
   snakes are there at the zoo?

   34   29   33

2. Bill's class read 12 books
   about the zoo.
   Jon's class read 11. How
   many books about the zoo
   did the two classes read?

   23   31   27

3. Mark took photos of
   13 animals. Neil took photos
   of 18 animals. How many
   photos of animals did the
   two boys take?

   32   28   31

4. Maria fed the elephant
   19 peanuts.
   Tim fed it 16 peanuts.
   How many peanuts did they
   feed the elephant?

   23   35   12

5. Jill bought 13 tiger erasers
   at the gift shop.
   Joan bought 16 monkey
   erasers.
   How many erasers did
   they buy?

   29   21   39

6. The petting zoo had 12 goats
   and 14 sheep.
   How many goats and sheep
   were there at the
   petting zoo?

   25   26   33

7. The snack shop sold 28 bags
   of peanuts. It sold 31 bags
   of popcorn. How many
   bags of popcorn and peanuts
   did the shop sell?

   28   59   31

8. Nico bought 14 bear stickers
   at the zoo.
   Hans bought 18 bird stickers
   How many stickers did
   they buy in all?

   18   22   32

Adding One-Digit and Two-Digit Numbers

Write the missing addend.

1.

$$\begin{array}{r} 5\ 7 \\ +\ 7 \\ \hline 6\ 4 \end{array}$$

$$\begin{array}{r} 6\ 4 \\ +\ \square \\ \hline 6\ 9 \end{array}$$

$$\begin{array}{r} 4\ 3 \\ +\ \square \\ \hline 5\ 0 \end{array}$$

$$\begin{array}{r} 6\ 5 \\ +\ \square \\ \hline 7\ 4 \end{array}$$
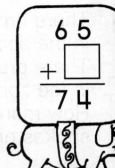

2.

$$\begin{array}{r} 7\ 6 \\ +\ \square \\ \hline 8\ 2 \end{array}$$
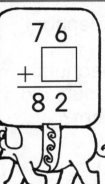

$$\begin{array}{r} 2\ 9 \\ +\ \square \\ \hline 3\ 2 \end{array}$$

$$\begin{array}{r} 3\ 0 \\ +\ \square \\ \hline 3\ 4 \end{array}$$

$$\begin{array}{r} 8\ 5 \\ +\ \square \\ \hline 9\ 4 \end{array}$$

3.

$$\begin{array}{r} 4\ 6 \\ +\ \square \\ \hline 5\ 4 \end{array}$$

$$\begin{array}{r} 5\ 3 \\ +\ \square \\ \hline 6\ 1 \end{array}$$

$$\begin{array}{r} 2\ 5 \\ +\ \square \\ \hline 3\ 2 \end{array}$$

$$\begin{array}{r} 1\ 3 \\ +\ \square \\ \hline 2\ 0 \end{array}$$

4.

$$\begin{array}{r} 6\ 3 \\ +\ \square \\ \hline 7\ 1 \end{array}$$
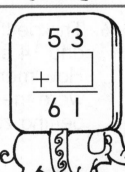

$$\begin{array}{r} 9\ 2 \\ +\ \square \\ \hline 9\ 9 \end{array}$$

$$\begin{array}{r} 7\ 4 \\ +\ \square \\ \hline 7\ 7 \end{array}$$

$$\begin{array}{r} 4\ 5 \\ +\ \square \\ \hline 5\ 1 \end{array}$$

Adding Two-Digit Numbers

Solve. Color the answer.

1. Joey had 75 cards.
   He bought 16 more.
   How many cards does he
   have in all?
   Color the answer blue.

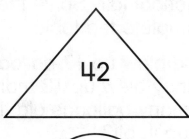

2. Felicia had 14 books.
   Latoya gave her 28 more.
   How many books does she
   have in all?
   Color the answer yellow.

3. Kenny had 27 marbles.
   Joey gave him 35 more.
   How many marbles does he
   have in all?
   Color the answer purple.

91

4. Ellen had 64 pencils.
   Tracy gave her 17 more.
   How many pencils does she
   have in all?
   Color the answer green.

5. Nadema had 46 stickers.
   Renaldo gave her 18 more.
   How many stickers does she
   have in all?
   Color the answer red.

81

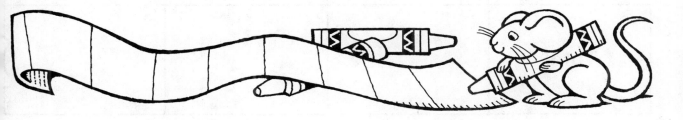

More About Two-Digit Addition

Angela and her friends blew up balloons
for the school fair. Solve the problems.
Then complete the table.

1. Angela blew up 17 balloons.
Courtney blew up 18 more.
How many balloons did they
blow up in all?

_____ balloons

2. Before lunch Jacob blew up
14 balloons. After lunch he
blew up 27 more. How many
balloons did he blow up in all?

_____ balloons

3. Courtney blew up 25 balloons.
She blew up 20 more. How
many balloons did she blow
up in all?

_____ balloons

4. Angela blew up 45 more
balloons. Jacob blew up 17.
How many more balloons did
they blow up in all?

_____ balloons

Write how many balloons each person blew up.

	Angela	Courtney	Jacob
Total			

Write the Addition Problem

Solve.

1. Thomas has 26 toy cars.
   Jack has 25 toy trucks.
   How many cars and trucks
   do they have?

   _____ cars and trucks

2. Anna picked 32 flowers.
   Liz picked 26 flowers.
   How many flowers did they
   pick in all?

   _____ flowers

3. Mark has 21 marbles.
   Tommy has 19 marbles.
   How many marbles do they
   have in all?

   _____ marbles

4. Sarah fed her dog 28 cans of
   dog food last month. Geno fed
   his dog 29 cans. How many
   cans of dog food did the two
   dogs eat last month?

   _____ cans

Problem Solving • Too Much Information

Make up a story problem with information that is not in
the picture. Have a friend find the information that is not needed.
Solve the problem together.

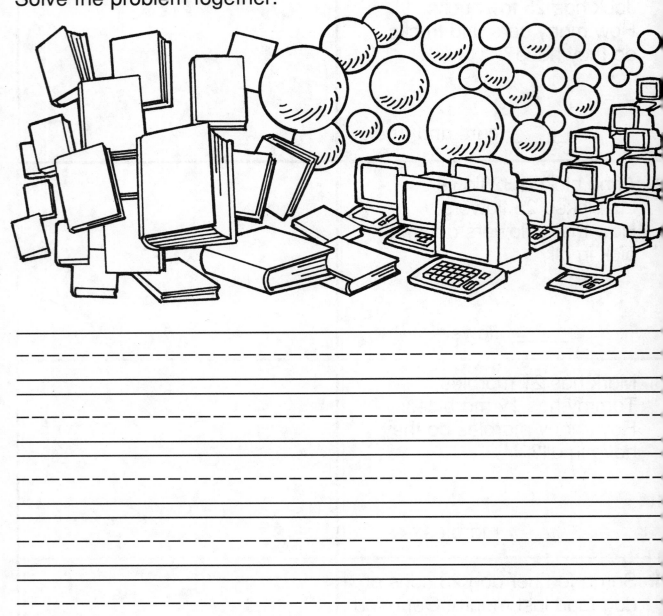

_____

- -

_____

- -

_____

- -

_____

- -

_____

- -

_____

- -

_____

- -

Names for Numbers

Write how many tens and ones after 1 ten is regrouped as 10 ones.

1. 46 _____ tens _____ 16 ones

2. 57 _____ tens _____ ones

3. 75 _____ tens _____ ones

4. 24 _____ ten _____ ones

5. 38 _____ tens _____ ones

6. 41 _____ tens _____ ones

7. 53 _____ tens _____ ones

8. 92 _____ tens _____ ones

9. 84 _____ tens _____ ones

10. 61 _____ tens _____ ones

11. 73 _____ tens _____ ones

12. 52 _____ tens _____ ones

13. 43 _____ tens _____ ones

14. 66 _____ tens _____ ones

Name_____

Modeling One-Digit
and Two-Digit Subtraction

Use Workmat 3 and base-ten blocks.
Subtract. Color the stop sign red
if you need to regroup.

1.

$$\begin{array}{r} \overset{3\ 16}{\cancel{46}} \\ -\ 8 \\ \hline 38 \end{array}$$

2.

$$\begin{array}{r} 29 \\ -\ 7 \\ \hline \end{array}$$

3.

$$\begin{array}{r} 37 \\ -\ 9 \\ \hline \end{array}$$

4.

$$\begin{array}{r} 14 \\ -\ 6 \\ \hline \end{array}$$

5.

$$\begin{array}{r} 49 \\ -\ 9 \\ \hline \end{array}$$

6.

$$\begin{array}{r} 24 \\ -\ 3 \\ \hline \end{array}$$

7.

$$\begin{array}{r} 16 \\ -\ 5 \\ \hline \end{array}$$

8.

$$\begin{array}{r} 34 \\ -\ 8 \\ \hline \end{array}$$

9.

$$\begin{array}{r} 19 \\ -\ 8 \\ \hline \end{array}$$

10.

$$\begin{array}{r} 26 \\ -\ 7 \\ \hline \end{array}$$

11.

$$\begin{array}{r} 18 \\ -\ 5 \\ \hline \end{array}$$

12.

$$\begin{array}{r} 32 \\ -\ 4 \\ \hline \end{array}$$

Recording Subtraction

Use Workmat 3 and base-ten blocks. Complete each table.

1.

Subtract 4.	
56	52
44	
35	

Subtract 6.	
37	
25	
17	

Subtract 8.	
50	
39	
28	

2.

Subtract 10.	
59	
40	
32	

Subtract 7.	
68	
52	
35	

Subtract 5.	
49	
35	
26	

3.

Subtract 3.	
29	
16	
12	

Subtract 9.	
69	
54	
40	

Subtract 2.	
31	
27	
10	

4.

Subtract 8.	
67	
28	
15	

Subtract 5.	
47	
31	
28	

Subtract 6.	
59	
42	
18	

Recording Two-Digit Subtraction

Subtract. Find the answer to the riddle.

What is the best way to call a dragon?

L			
19	9	15	11

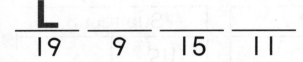

| 26 | 18 | 4 | 17 | 13 | 15 | 14 | 7 | 29 |

A	C	D	E
35 − 22	28 − 14	48 − 22	19 − 12

G	I	L	N
27 − 16	51 − 33	44 − 25 19	43 − 28

O	S	T	!
25 − 16	26 − 22	44 − 27	48 − 19

Problem Solving • Choose the Operation

Circle the question that completes the problem.
Then write **+** or **−** and solve.

1. There are 32 goldfish
in a fish tank.
Nick buys 14 of them.

(How many fish are
left?)

How many fish are
there in all?

$$\begin{array}{r} \overset{2\ 12}{\cancel{32}} \\ \ominus\ 14 \\ \hline 18 \end{array}$$

___18___ goldfish

2. Sam has 60¢.
His mother gives him
30¢ more.

How much money
is left?

How much money does
Sam have in all?

$$\begin{array}{r} 60¢ \\ \bigcirc\ 30¢ \\ \hline \end{array}$$

_____ ¢

3. Amanda has 75¢.
She buys 2 cookies that
cost 43¢.

How much money
does she have in all?

How much money
does she have left?

$$\begin{array}{r} 75¢ \\ \bigcirc\ 43¢ \\ \hline \end{array}$$

_____ ¢

4. Megan has 25 stickers
at home. She gets
20 more at the store.

How many stickers
does she have in all?

How many stickers
does she have left?

$$\begin{array}{r} 20 \\ \bigcirc\ 25 \\ \hline \end{array}$$

_____ stickers

5. Tricia has 54 pennies.
Her father gives her
29 more pennies.

How many pennies
does she have left?

How many pennies
does she have in all?

$$\begin{array}{r} 54¢ \\ \bigcirc\ 29¢ \\ \hline \end{array}$$

_____ pennies

6. Logan has 95 marbles.
He gives 26 marbles
to John.

How many marbles does
Logan have in all?

How many marbles
does Logan have left?

$$\begin{array}{r} 95 \\ \bigcirc\ 26 \\ \hline \end{array}$$

_____ marbles

Subtracting One-Digit from Two-Digit Numbers

Subtract. How many ones are left?
Find the color for that many ones.
Use it to color that animal in the picture.

0 ones	white	3 ones	brown
1 one	pink	4 ones	black
2 ones	white	5 ones	red

$43 - 9 =$ _____

$89 - 8 =$ _____

$77 - 7 =$ _____

$60 - 5 =$ _____

$31 - 9 =$ _____

$22 - 9 =$ _____

Two-Digit Subtraction

Subtract. Color the circle in which you regrouped.
Then write the names of the holidays.

1.

76
− 29

Kwanzaa

92
− 81

Monday

51
− 6

Presidents Day

40
− 28

Veterans Day

2.

33
− 3

Tuesday

63
− 17

Thanksgiving

85
− 42

Wednesday

47
− 8

Independence Day

3.

36
− 9

Columbus Day

25
− 14

Thursday

14
− 11

Friday

29
− 8

Saturday

Happy Holidays

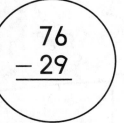 K _____

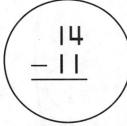 T _____

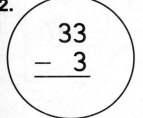 P _____

 I _____

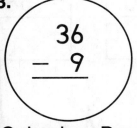 V _____

C _____

Practicing Two-Digit Subtraction

Which way should K.C. go to get to the tree?
He must take the path with answers greater than 40.
Subtract. Then draw a line to show the correct path!

$$\begin{array}{r} 91 \\ -\ 33 \\ \hline \end{array}$$

$$\begin{array}{r} 76 \\ -\ 21 \\ \hline \end{array}$$

$$\begin{array}{r} 93 \\ -\ 69 \\ \hline \end{array}$$

$$\begin{array}{r} 93 \\ -\ 37 \\ \hline \end{array}$$

$$\begin{array}{r} 43 \\ -\ 26 \\ \hline \end{array}$$

$$\begin{array}{r} 81 \\ -\ 73 \\ \hline \end{array}$$

$$\begin{array}{r} 78 \\ -\ 59 \\ \hline \end{array}$$

$$\begin{array}{r} 62 \\ -\ 20 \\ \hline \end{array}$$

$$\begin{array}{r} 87 \\ -\ 56 \\ \hline \end{array}$$

$$\begin{array}{r} 66 \\ -\ 25 \\ \hline \end{array}$$

$$\begin{array}{r} 43 \\ -\ 27 \\ \hline \end{array}$$

$$\begin{array}{r} 59 \\ -\ 14 \\ \hline \end{array}$$

House of Numbers

Add or subtract. Use your answers to complete the puzzle.

Across

1.
$$\begin{array}{r} {\scriptstyle 1} \\ 34 \\ +28 \\ \hline 62 \end{array}$$

3.
$$\begin{array}{r} 58 \\ +33 \\ \hline \end{array}$$

6.
$$\begin{array}{r} 29 \\ +29 \\ \hline \end{array}$$

7.
$$\begin{array}{r} 19 \\ +33 \\ \hline \end{array}$$

8.
$$\begin{array}{r} 42 \\ +21 \\ \hline \end{array}$$

Down

2.
$$\begin{array}{r} 54 \\ -25 \\ \hline \end{array}$$

4.
$$\begin{array}{r} 36 \\ -19 \\ \hline \end{array}$$

5.
$$\begin{array}{r} 40 \\ -16 \\ \hline \end{array}$$

6.
$$\begin{array}{r} 66 \\ -15 \\ \hline \end{array}$$

7.
$$\begin{array}{r} 81 \\ -28 \\ \hline \end{array}$$

Problem Solving • Choose the Operation

Use the picture. Solve.

1. Sammy has 85¢. If he buys
   [COLORS] and [kite], how much
   money will he have left?

   _____ ¢

2. Karla has 90¢. If she buys
   [apple] and [boots], how much
   money will she have left?

   _____ ¢

3. Robin has 99¢. She spent 88¢ for
   a [clown] and [COLORS]. How much more
   does she need to buy a [kite]?

   _____ ¢

4. Ben has 95¢. He spent 57¢ for
   a [kite] and [apple]. How much more
   does he need to buy [boots]?

   _____ ¢

Tally Tables

Look at the picture. Fill in the tally table.

The Circus		
I.	🐘	
2.	🐩	
3.	🐴	
4.	🤡	

Write 3 questions about this table.
Give your questions to a classmate to answer.

_____

- -

_____

- -

_____

- -

Problem Solving • Use a Table

Read the statements.
Cut out the boxes of tally marks.
Paste the boxes in the correct space.

1. Only one person wanted a banana.

2. Twice as many people wanted grapes as bananas.

3. Two more people wanted apples rather than bananas.

4. Five people wanted watermelon.

5. The number of people wanting oranges was one less than those wanting watermelon.

I	III	II
ЖH	IIII	

Taking a Survey

Ask 10 classmates these questions.

1. Do you like hamburgers or hot dogs better?

hamburgers	
hot dogs	

2. Do you like mustard, mayonnaise, or ketchup best?

mustard	
mayonnaise	
ketchup	

3. Do you like chips or french fries with your hamburger or hot dog?

chips	
french fries	

Write two things you learned from your survey.

4. _____
   _____
   _____

5. _____
   _____
   _____

Comparing Data in Tables

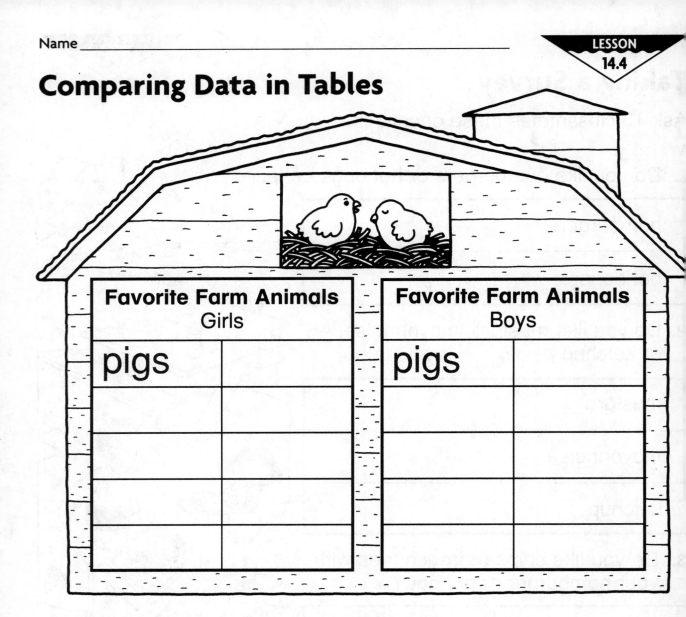

Favorite Farm Animals Girls	
pigs	

Favorite Farm Animals Boys	
pigs	

Complete the tally tables by reading the sentences.

1. The girls gave the pigs 2 votes.
   The boys gave the pigs I less vote.

2. The boys gave the cows 3 votes.
   The girls gave the cows twice as many votes as the boys.

3. The hens got 5 votes from the boys.
   The hens got I less vote from the girls than the boys.

4. The girls gave the horses I vote.
   The horses got twice as many votes from the boys as the girls.

5. The boys gave the ducks 5 votes. They gave the hens the same number of votes. The girls gave the ducks 3 votes.

Picture Graphs

The graph shows what Heather and David saw
when they looked at the night sky in July.

Night Sky In July	
full moon	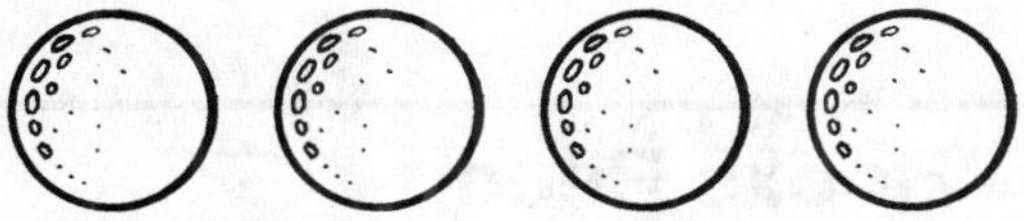 🌕 🌕 🌕 🌕
half moon	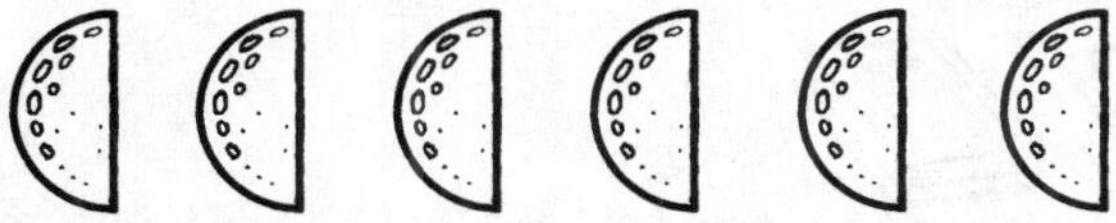 🌗 🌗 🌗 🌗 🌗 🌗
crescent moon	 🌙 🌙 🌙 🌙 🌙 🌙
clouds	 ☁ ☁ ☁ ☁ ☁ ☁ ☁ ☁ ☁ ☁

Write questions about the graph.
Give them to a classmate to answer.

_____

_____

_____

_____

_____

_____

_____

_____

_____

_____

_____

_____

_____

_____

Pictographs

You will need: calculator

This graph shows how many books were read by each child in March. The child who read the most books won a ribbon.

Books Read	
Maria	📖 📖
Jesse	📖 📖 📖 📖 📖
Bill	📖 📖 📖 📖
Candi	📖 📖 📖

Each 📖 stands for 6 books.

1. How many books did Bill read? _____ books

2. How many books did Candi read? _____ books

3. How many more books did Bill read than Maria? _____ books

4. How many books did Maria and Jesse read altogether? _____ books

5. How many books did the winner read? _____ books

6. How many fewer books did Candi read than Jesse? _____ books

7. Who read fewer than 18 books? _____

orizontal Bar Graphs

This bar graph shows how many leaves children collected for a science project.

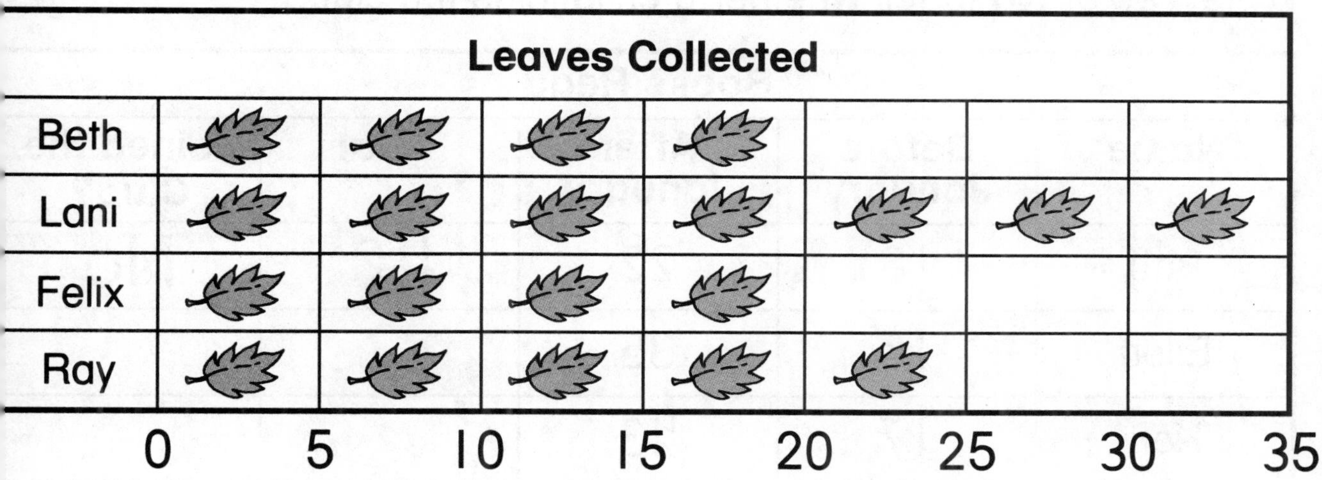

Leaves Collected

Beth	🍂	🍂	🍂	🍂			
Lani	🍂	🍂	🍂	🍂	🍂	🍂	🍂
Felix	🍂	🍂	🍂	🍂			
Ray	🍂	🍂	🍂	🍂	🍂		

0   5   10   15   20   25   30   35

. How many leaves did Beth collect?   _____ leaves

2. How many more leaves did Lani
collect than Felix?   _____ more leaves

3. How many leaves did Beth and Ray
collect altogether?   _____ leaves

4. How many leaves did Lani and Felix
collect altogether?   _____ leaves

5. Make up a question about the graph. Give it to a classmate to answer.

_____

_____

_____

_____

_____

_____

Problem Solving • Make a Graph

Children in Mrs. Webb's class who read 50 books join the
50 Book Club. Add.
Write **Yes** or **No** to tell whether a child joins the club.

Books Read				
Name	Before January	After January	Total	Joined the Club?
Bob	18	22	40	No
Ellen	15	35		
Ken	17	43		
Joan	29	21		
Amy	18	12		

Color the graph to show how many
books each child read.

Books Read						
Bob						
Ellen						
Ken						
Joan						
Amy						

0   10   20   30   40   50   6

Certain or Impossible

Look at the animals. Draw pictures of farm
animals that you are certain could come out of the barn. Then
draw animals that are impossible to come out of the barn.

Certain   **Impossible**

Interpreting Outcomes of Games

Work with a partner.
You will need: 7 blue cubes, 3 red cubes, 1 bag

Put the cubes in the bag.
Take turns drawing a cube from the bag.
Put the cube back in the bag after each turn.
Draw 20 times.
Tally the cubes when pulled from the bag.

Color	Tally Marks
blue	
red	

1. What colors could be pulled from the bag?

_____   _____

_____ and _____

_____

2. Which color was pulled out more often? _____

3. Which color was pulled out less often? _____

4. Why do you think you pulled one color out more often than the other?

_____

_____

_____

_____

Most Likely

Work with a partner.
You will need: 8 red tiles, 2 yellow tiles, 1 blue tile, 1 bag

1. Put all the tiles in a bag. Pull out 1 tile. Make a tally mark to show which color you pulled out.

2. Put the tile back in the bag. Shake. Take turns. Do this 9 more times.

Color	Tally Marks
red	
yellow	
blue	

3. Make a prediction. If you do this 10 more times, which color do you think you will pull out most often? _____

4. Why do you think this will happen?

_____

_____

5. Check your prediction. Do this 10 more times. Explain what happened.

_____

_____

_____

_____

Less Likely

Work with a partner.
You will need: 8 red cubes, 8 blue cubes, 1 bag

1. Put the cubes in your bag so that you will pull red
   less often than blue.

   Write how many red. _____   Write how many blue. _____

   Put the cubes in the bag. Take turns pulling out 1 cube.
   Make a tally mark each time.

Color	Tally Marks
red	
blue	

2. Put the cubes in your bag so that you will pull blue
   less often than red.

   Write how many red. _____   Write how many blue. _____

   Put the cubes in the bag. Take turns pulling out 1 cube.
   Make a tally mark each time.

Color	Tally Marks
red	
blue	

3. Look at both tables.
   Explain what happened. _____

_____

_____

Identifying Solids

Cross out the solid figure that does not belong.

Sorting Solid Figures

Cross out the stacks that could not be made.

1.

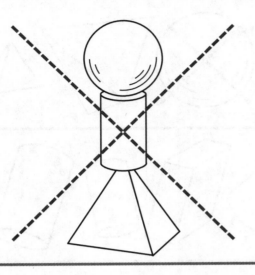

2.

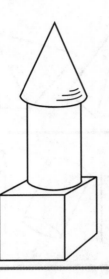

3.

4.

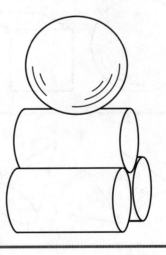

5.

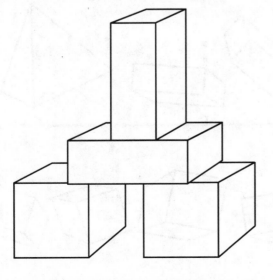

6.

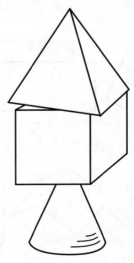

roblem Solving • Look for a Pattern

Work with a partner.
Color the figures in the top row to make a pattern.
Then have your partner color the figures in the bottom
ow to make a different pattern.

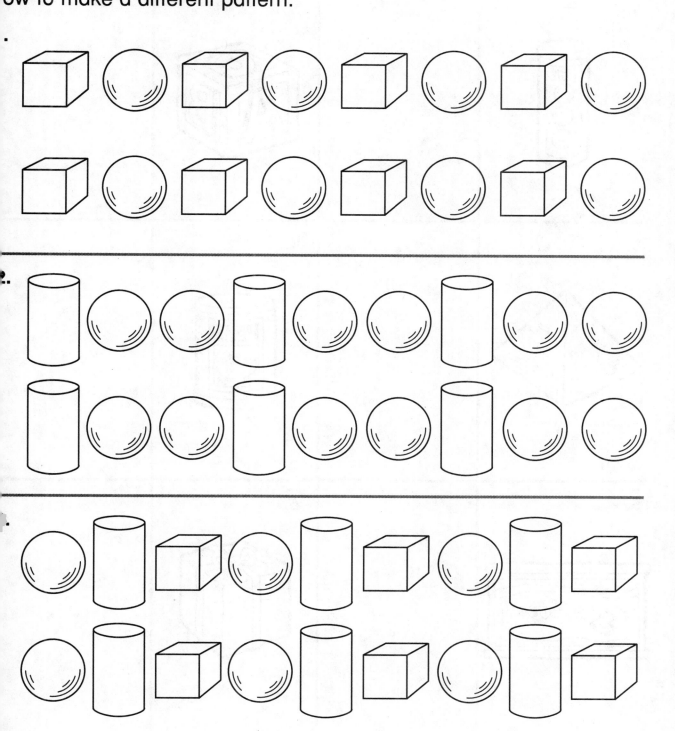

Making Plane Figures

Draw the part of the shape you could trace.

1.

2.

3.

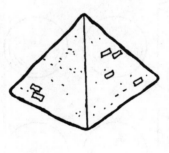

4.

5.

6.

Plane Figures

Draw a picture using squares, triangles, circles and rectangles.

How many △? _____   How many ☐? _____

How many ◯? _____   How many ▭? _____

Sides and Corners

Look at the figures in each row.
Find two figures whose dashed sides are
the same length. Circle those figures.

1.

2.

 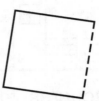

3.

4.

 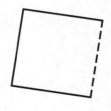

5.

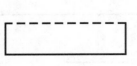 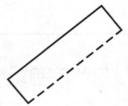  

Separating to Make New Figures

Work with a partner. Each use a different color.
Draw lines to make triangles in the square.
Do not make any triangles overlap.

Use tally marks to record the triangles you made.

My △ s.	
Your △ s.	

Congruent Figures

Find figures in the picture that are the
same size and shape as the ones in the box.
Number them to match.

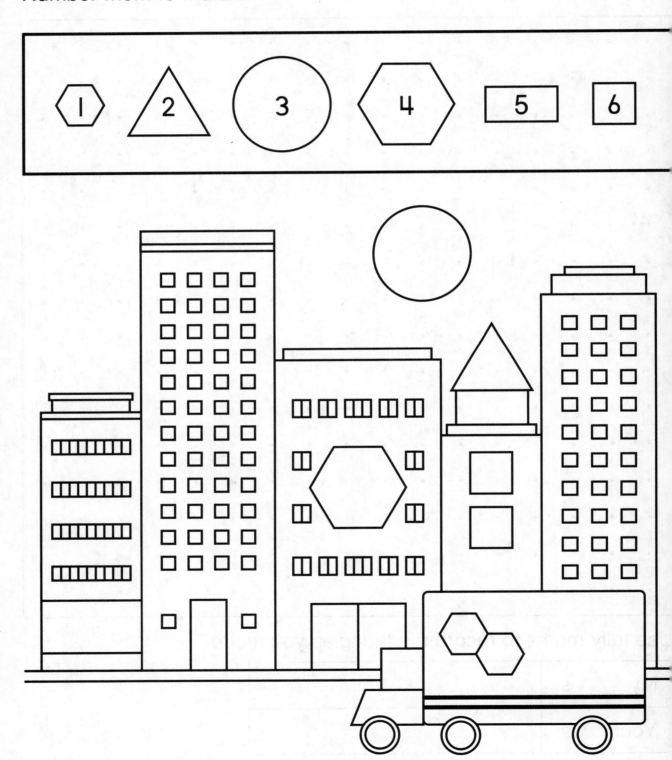

Line of Symmetry

Find the things in the picture that have symmetry.
Draw the line of symmetry. Color the picture.

More Symmetry

Draw one line of symmetry when you can.
Draw two lines of symmetry when you can.
Some letters have no lines of symmetry.

1.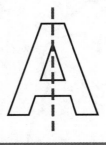

2.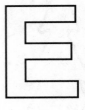

3.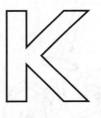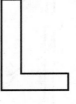

4.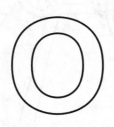

5.

Moving Figures

Cut out the figures to fit the puzzle.

Write how many of each figure
it takes to fill the rectangle.

____   ____   ____

More About Moving Figures

You will need a small square attribute block.
Move the block on the grid.
Color the squares as directed.

green

		Start here		

1. Color the starting square green.

2. Slide one to the right and down one.
   Color that square and 2 squares to the left green.

3. Slide one to the right and down one.
   Color that row green.

4. Slide down one. Color that row green.

5. Flip down one. Slide two to the left.
   Color the square brown.

Using Nonstandard Units

Estimate how many cubes long each one is.
Then measure with cubes to check your estimate.

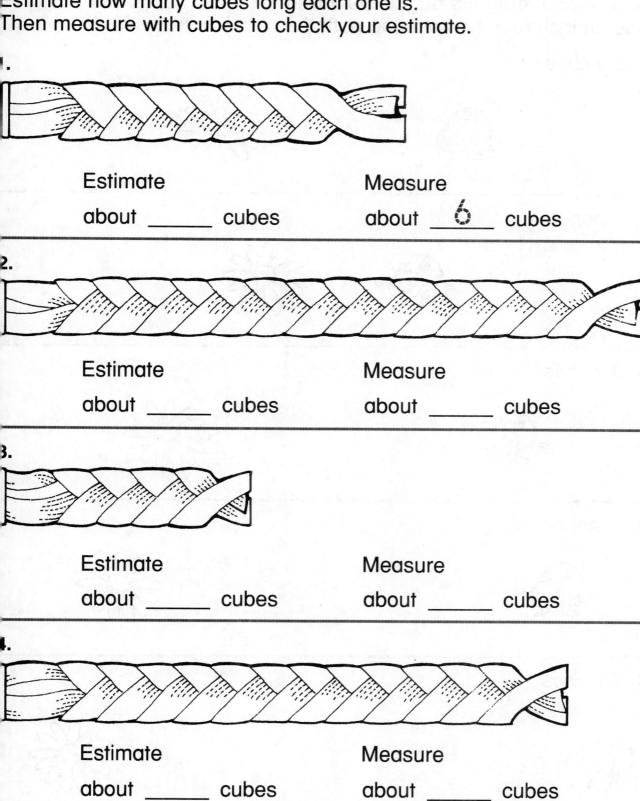

1.

Estimate

about _____ cubes

Measure

about __6__ cubes

2.

Estimate

about _____ cubes

Measure

about _____ cubes

3.

Estimate

about _____ cubes

Measure

about _____ cubes

4.

Estimate

about _____ cubes

Measure

about _____ cubes

Measuring with Inch Units

Draw a path from the bug to the flower.
Use an inch ruler to make the path the right length.

1. 2 inches

2. 1 inch

3. 3 inches

4. 4 inches

5. 5 inches

Using an Inch Ruler

Work with a friend.
Number the objects in order from shortest to longest.
Estimate how long each one is.
Then find and measure each object.

	Estimate Number of inches	Measure Number of inches
1. _____	_____	_____
2. _____	_____	_____
3. _____	_____	_____
4. _____	_____	_____
5. _____	_____	_____

Inch or Foot

Think of the real object.
Circle the better unit to measure each object.

1.

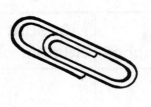

(inch)
foot

2.

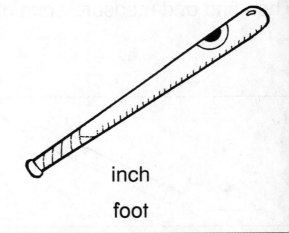

inch
foot

3.

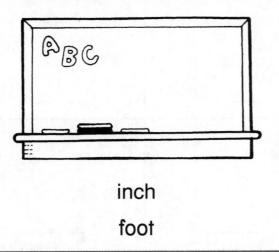

inch

foot

4.

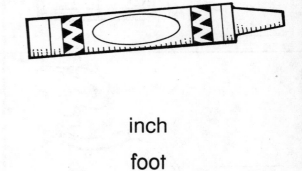

inch

foot

5.

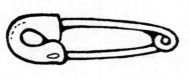

inch

foot

6.

inch

foot

Name _____

LESSON 20.5

Problem Solving • Guess and Check

Write the letter.
Guess which path is longest.

Guess which path is shortest.

_____

_____

To check, put yarn along the path and measure the yarn.
Write the letter.

the longest path _____

the shortest path _____

STRETCH YOUR THINKING   E107

Centimeters

1. Draw a path between two dots that is 8 centimeters long.

2. Draw a path between two dots that is 6 centimeters long.

3. Draw a path between two dots that is longer than
   3 centimeters but shorter than 5 centimeters.

4. Draw a path between two dots that is longer than
   10 centimeters but shorter than 12 centimeters.

Decimeters as a Ruler

Measure and cut a string that is 1 decimeter
long. Work with a friend. Use the string
to find things in your classroom that are
longer and shorter than 1 decimeter.
Write the names of the things you found.

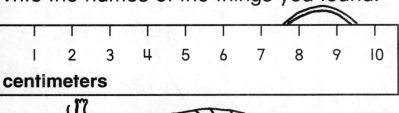

| 1 | 2 | 3 | 4 | 5 | 6 | 7 | 8 | 9 | 10 |
centimeters

longer	shorter
_____	_____
_____	_____
_____	_____
_____	_____
_____	_____
_____	_____
_____	_____
_____	_____
_____	_____
_____	_____
_____	_____

Exploring Perimeter

Use your centimeter ruler to draw
figures with the following perimeters.
Write the length of each side.

1. 8 centimeters

2. 15 centimeters

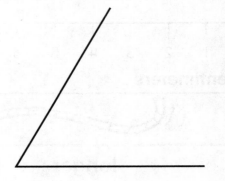

3. 12 centimeters

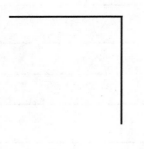

4. 24 centimeters

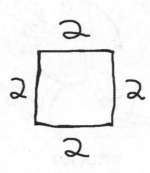

5. 11 centimeters

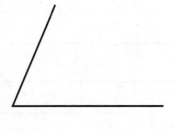

6. 19 centimeters

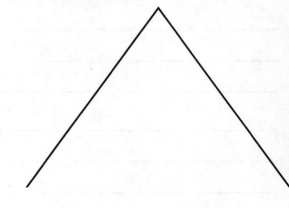

Problem Solving • Guess and Check

You need pattern blocks.

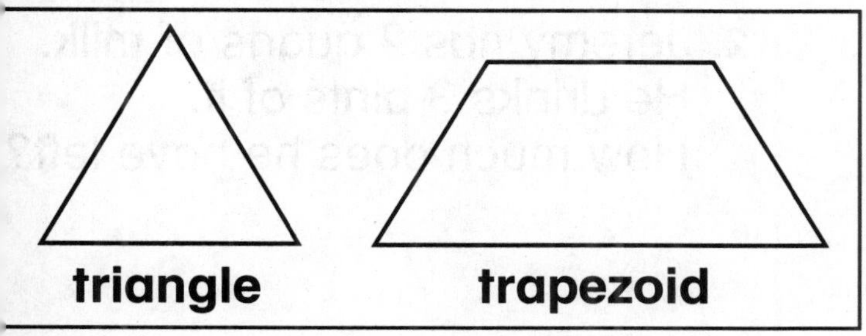

triangle   trapezoid

Use △. Then use ⬠ .
Guess how many will fit in the figure.
Then use your pattern blocks to check.

1.

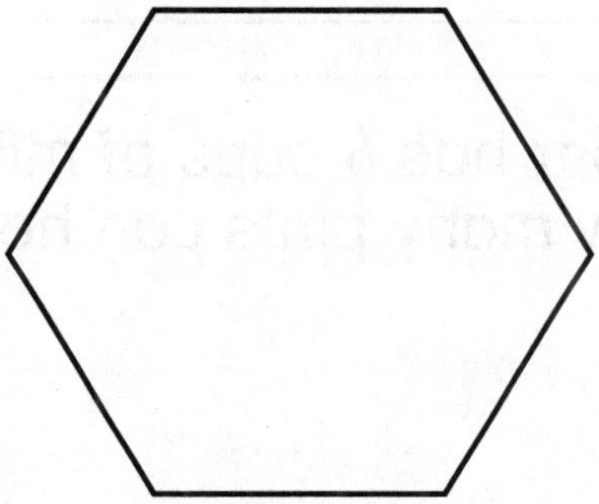

Guess _____ △

Measure _____ △

2.

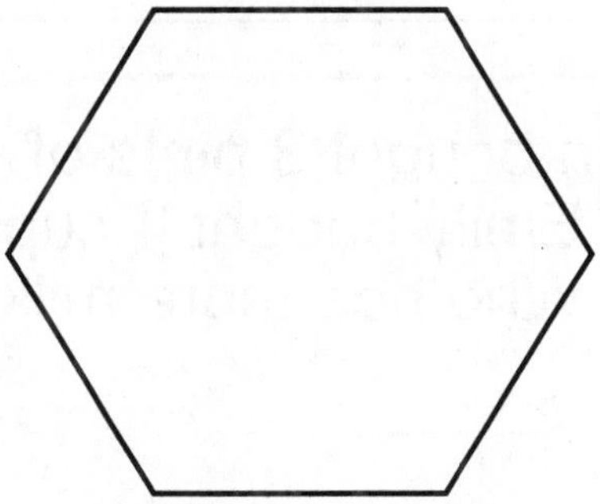

Guess _____ ⬠

Measure _____ ⬠

3.

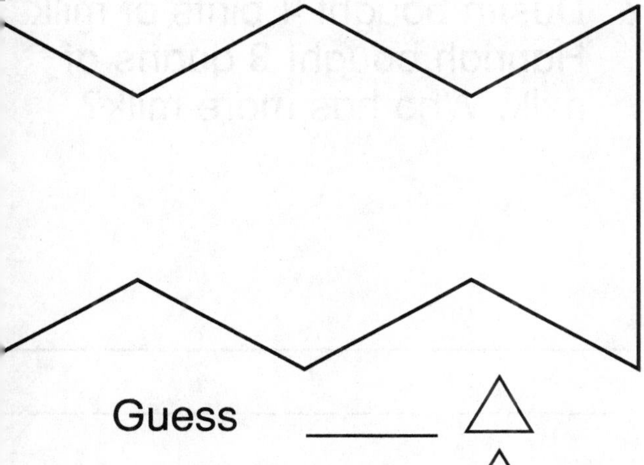

Guess _____ △

Measure _____ △

4.

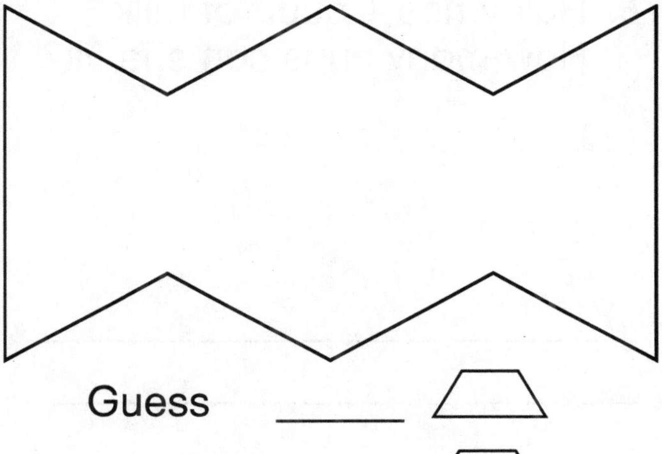

Guess _____ ⬠

Measure _____ ⬠

Using Cups, Pints, and Quarts

Solve.

1. Tamala has 4 cups of milk.
   Glen has 1 pint of milk.
   Who has more milk?

   _____
   - - - - - - - - - - - - - - -
   _____

2. Jeremy has 2 quarts of milk.
   He drinks 3 pints of it.
   How much does he have left?

   _____
   - - - - - - - - - - - - - - -
   _____

3. Delsin bought 3 pints of
   milk. Emily bought 4 cups of
   milk. Who has more milk?

   _____
   - - - - - - - - - - - - - - -
   _____

4. Cesar has 6 cups of milk.
   How many pints can he fill?

   _____
   - - - - - - - - - - - - - - -
   _____

5. Haley has 1 quart of milk.
   How many cups can she fill?

   _____
   - - - - - - - - - - - - - - -
   _____

6. Dustin bought 4 pints of milk.
   Hannah bought 3 quarts of
   milk. Who has more milk?

   _____
   - - - - - - - - - - - - - - -
   _____

More or Less than a Pound

weighs about 1 ounce

weighs about 1 pound

Does the object weigh
nearer to an **ounce** or a **pound?**
Circle the correct answer.

1.

(ounce)   pound

ounce   pound

ounce   pound

2.

ounce   pound

ounce   pound

ounce   pound

3.

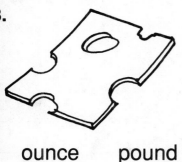

ounce   pound

ounce   pound

ounce   pound

Using a Thermometer

Color to show the temperature.
Then draw a picture to show something
you like to do when it is 80°F.

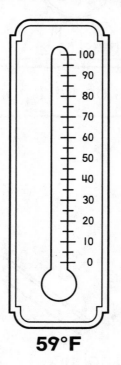

59°F

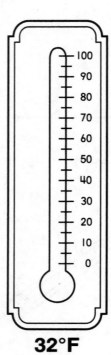

32°F

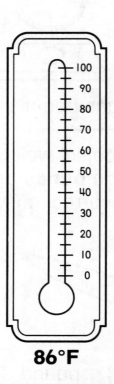

86°F

Choosing the Appropriate Tool

Work with a friend.
Write some things you can measure with each tool.

1.	2.	3.
cup	ruler	balance scale

Halves and Fourths

Divide the figure and color the parts.

1.

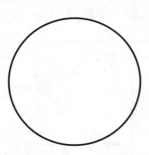

$\frac{1}{4}$ | red | $\frac{1}{4}$ | yellow |

$\frac{1}{4}$ | blue | $\frac{1}{4}$ | green |

2.

$\frac{1}{2}$ | green |

$\frac{1}{2}$ | yellow |

3.

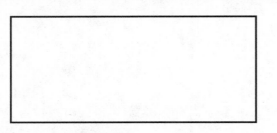

$\frac{1}{4}$ | orange | $\frac{1}{4}$ | yellow |

$\frac{1}{4}$ | red | $\frac{1}{4}$ | blue |

4.

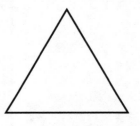

$\frac{1}{2}$ | purple |

$\frac{1}{2}$ | pink |

5.

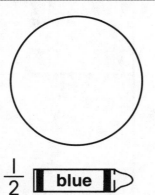

$\frac{1}{2}$ | blue |

$\frac{1}{2}$ | green |

6.

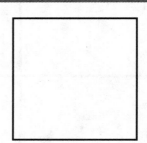

$\frac{1}{4}$ | brown | $\frac{1}{4}$ | green |

$\frac{1}{4}$ | orange | $\frac{1}{4}$ | purple |

Name _____

Thirds and Sixths

Divide each figure into halves, fourths, thirds, or sixths.
Color one part. Write the fraction.

1.

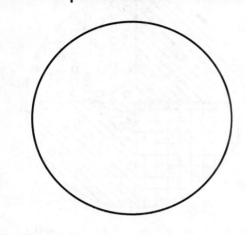

2.

3.

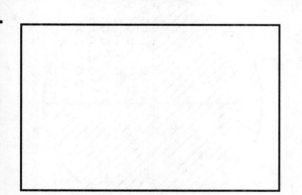

4.

More About Fractions

Write the fraction.

1.

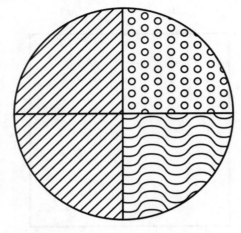

What fraction of the circle
is ?

2.

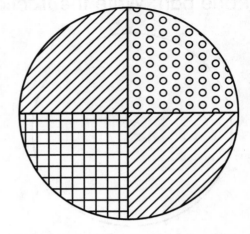

What fraction of the circle
is 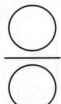?

3.

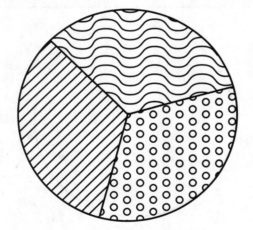

What fraction of the circle
is ?

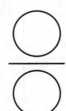

4.

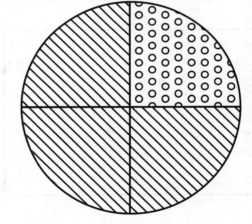

What fraction of the circle
is ?

Parts of Groups

Use the picture to answer the questions.

1.

What fraction of the
cats have spots?

—
◯

What fraction of the
cats are white?

—
◯

2.

What fraction of the
dogs have long tails?

—
◯

What fraction of the
dogs have short tails?

—
◯

3.

What fraction of the
rabbits are sitting?

—
◯

What fraction of the
rabbits are jumping?

—
◯

4.

What fraction of the
fish are small?

—
◯

What fraction of the
fish have stripes?

—
◯

STRETCH YOUR THINKING   E119

Problem Solving • Make a Model

Draw a picture to solve the problem.
Circle the answer.

1. Sonya made a pizza with 6 slices. She put pepperoni on $\frac{2}{6}$ of the pizza. She put hamburger on $\frac{3}{6}$ of the pizza. She put black olives on $\frac{1}{6}$ of the pizza. Which did she have the most of on her pizza, pepperoni, hamburger, or black olives?

pepperoni

hamburger

black olives

2. Henry had $\frac{1}{4}$ red gum balls. He had $\frac{2}{4}$ yellow gum balls. He had $\frac{1}{4}$ blue gum balls. Did Henry have more red, yellow, or blue gum balls?

red gum balls

yellow gum balls

blue gum balls

Groups of Hundreds

Write the number. Then write < or >.

1.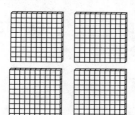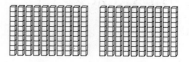

_____   _____

2.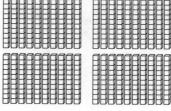

_____   _____

3.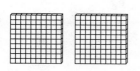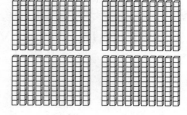

_____   _____

4.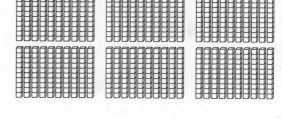

_____   _____

5.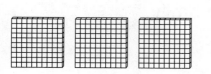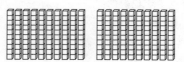

_____   _____

Numbers to 500

Circle the reasonable answer.

1. Annie is _____ years older than Maggie.

(2)   100   200

2. There are _____ seats in the circus tent.

1   10   100

3. There are _____ children in this class.

3   30   300

4. There are _____ pages in the dictionary.

8   80   800

5. Mark is 6 years old. His brother is _____ years old.

9   90   900

6. Nikki has _____ sisters.

4   40   400

7. The kickball team has _____ members.

1   10   100

8. The United States flag has _____ stars.

5   50   500

9. There are _____ children in the school.

2   20   200

10. There are _____ children in the family.

3   30   300

Numbers to 1,000

Use the clues to find the number.

1. This number has an 8 in the hundreds place.

   The tens place has 2 less than the hundreds place.

   The ones place has 3 more than the tens place.

   What is the number? _869_

2. This number has a 3 in the hundreds place.

   The tens place has 3 more than the hundreds place.

   The ones place has 1 less than the tens place.

   What is the number? _____

3. This number has a 5 in the hundreds place.

   The tens place has 4 less than the hundreds place.

   The ones place has 3 more than the tens place.

   What is the number? _____

4. This number has a 1 in the hundreds place.

   The tens place has 5 more than the hundreds place.

   The ones place has 2 more than the tens place.

   What is the number? _____

5. This number has a 2 in the hundreds place.

   The tens place has 6 more than the hundreds place.

   The ones place has 4 less than the tens place.

   What is the number? _____

6. This number has a 4 in the hundreds place.

   The tens place has 1 less than the hundreds place.

   The ones place has 1 less than the tens place.

   What is the number? _____

Use a Model

Look at the model. Read the problem.
Change the model to answer the question.

1.

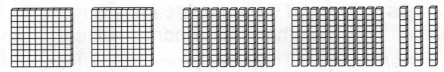

If this model showed 3 more tens, what number would the model

show? _____

2.

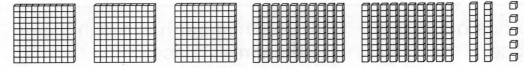

If this model showed 4 more ones and 7 more tens, what number

would the model show? _____

3.

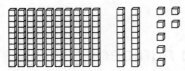

If this model showed 3 more tens and I less hundred, what number

would the model show? _____

4.

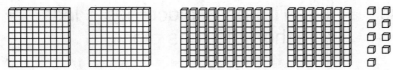

If this model showed I more one, what number would the model

show? _____

Building $1.00

Follow the path.
Stop at each tree and circle the greater amount.

Greater Than

Use Workmat 5. Read the problem.
Write the answers.

1. Put 4 hundreds, 2 tens, and
5 ones on your workmat.
What is that number?

$$425$$

Take off 2 tens.
Put on 3 ones and
4 hundreds. What is
the new number?

_____

Which number is
greater?

_____

2. Put 6 hundreds, I ten, and
4 ones on your workmat.
What is that number?

_____

Take off 2 hundreds.
Put on 8 tens and
4 ones. What is
the new number?

_____

Which number is
greater?

_____

3. Put 3 tens, 2 hundreds, and
5 ones on your workmat.
What is that number?

_____

Take off 3 tens.
Put on 4 ones. Take
off I hundred. What is
the new number?

_____

Which number is
greater?

_____

4. Put 9 ones, 9 tens, and
8 hundreds on your workmat
What is that number?

_____

Put on I hundred.
Take off 2 tens.
What is the new
number?

_____

Which number is
greater?

_____

Less Than

Compare the two numbers.
Circle the number that is less.
Write the correct letter in the boxes below.

1. $\frac{476}{L}$ $\frac{(475)}{Y}$		**2.** $\frac{191}{T}$ $\frac{119}{O}$	
3. $\frac{316}{M}$ $\frac{315}{U}$		**4.** $\frac{399}{O}$ $\frac{391}{G}$	
5. $\frac{249}{O}$ $\frac{250}{S}$		**6.** $\frac{555}{T}$ $\frac{565}{P}$	
7. $\frac{899}{I}$ $\frac{900}{F}$		**8.** $\frac{747}{R}$ $\frac{746}{T}$	

Y										!
1.	2.	3.		4.	5.	6.		7.	8.	

Name ______________________________

LESSON 25.3

Greater Than and Less Than

Use a number cube.
Roll three times to build a three-digit number.
Write that number.
Then write > or < in the circle.

1. 475 ◯ ____	2. ____ ◯ 115
3. 719 ◯ ____	4. 839 ◯ ____
5. 215 ◯ ____	6. ____ ◯ 346
7. ____ ◯ 145	8. 386 ◯ ____
9. ____ ◯ 272	10. 495 ◯ ____
11. ____ ◯ 321	12. ____ ◯ 528
13. 600 ◯ ____	14. 701 ◯ ____

Missing Numbers

Work with a friend.
Read the problem.
Find the number in the cloud.
Write the answer.

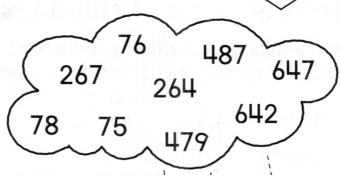

76   487
267   647
264
78   75   642
479

1. The number comes between 259 and 270.
   It is greater than 265.
   It is less than 268.
   The number is _____.

2. The number is greater than 77.
   It is between 70 and 80.

   The number is _____.

3. The number comes between 476 and 486.
   It is less than 484.
   It is greater than 478.
   The number is _____.

4. The number is less than 645.
   It is greater than 635.
   It is between 641 and 643.
   The number is _____.

5. The number is greater than 72.
   It is less than 78.
   It is between 74 and 76.

   The number is _____.

Ordering Sets of Numbers

Use a calculator. Write the answers.
Write the numbers in order from least to greatest.

1. $165 + 15 =$ _____

$180 - 20 =$ _____   _____ , _____ , _____

$180 - 40 =$ _____

2. $416 - 26 =$ _____

$500 - 30 =$ _____   _____ , _____ , _____

$405 + 76 =$ _____

3. $719 + 65 =$ _____

$113 + 675 =$ _____   _____ , _____ , _____

$326 + 15 =$ _____

4. $235 - 160 =$ _____

$145 + 409 =$ _____   _____ , _____ , _____

$535 + 16 =$ _____

5. $826 - 421 =$ _____

$534 - 156 =$ _____   _____ , _____ , _____

$392 + 106 =$ _____

Modeling Addition of Three-Digit Numbers

Use the table. Write the addition problem.

Flowers Planted	
tulips	241
roses	105
daisies	426
sunflowers	190
lilies	369

1.
sunflowers   _____
daisies   + _____
              _____

2.
tulips   _____
lilies   + _____
           _____

3.
lilies   _____
roses   + _____
           _____

4.
sunflowers   _____
tulips   + _____
              _____

5.
daisies   _____
roses   + _____
            _____

6.
lilies   _____
sunflowers + _____
              _____

Adding Three-Digit Numbers

Add.
Complete the chart.

1.

Add 123.	
341	464
564	
827	

2.

Add 341.	
265	
436	
647	

3.

Add 256.	
134	
523	
712	

4.

Add 415.	
337	
546	
272	

5.

Add 219.	
672	
561	
450	

6.

Add 143.	
427	
836	
717	

7.

Add 361.	
136	
247	
621	

8.

Add 422.	
575	
481	
366	

Modeling Subtraction of Three-Digit Numbers

Subtract. Then find the difference at the bottom.
Write its letter in the box. Read the secret message.

1.
```
   6 13
  2̶7̶3̶
- 116
-----
  157
```

2.
```
  426
- 119
-----
```

3.
```
  547
- 228
-----
```

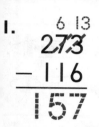

Y					

4.
```
  871
- 223
-----
```

5.
```
  653
- 419
-----
```

6.
```
  361
- 138
-----
```

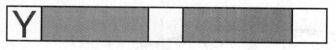

7.
```
  883
- 349
-----
```

8.
```
  863
- 618
-----
```

9.
```
  975
- 327
-----
```

10.
```
  670
- 436
-----
```

11.
```
  524
- 509
-----
```


A = 648	M = 245	O = 307
E = 223	S = 534	U = 319
T = 15	R = 234	Y = 157

Subtracting Three-Digit Numbers

Subtract.
How many hundreds are in the difference?
Find the color for that many hundreds.
Use it to color that part of the picture.

0 hundreds [red]	2 hundreds [blue]	4 hundreds [orange]
1 hundred [yellow]	3 hundreds [green]	5 hundreds [purple]

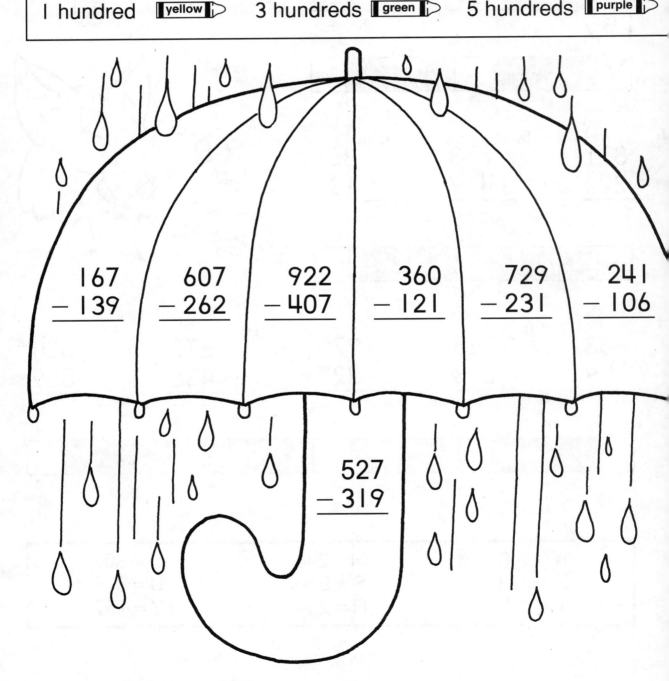

$$\begin{array}{r}167\\-139\\\hline\end{array}$$
$$\begin{array}{r}607\\-262\\\hline\end{array}$$
$$\begin{array}{r}922\\-407\\\hline\end{array}$$
$$\begin{array}{r}360\\-121\\\hline\end{array}$$
$$\begin{array}{r}729\\-231\\\hline\end{array}$$
$$\begin{array}{r}241\\-106\\\hline\end{array}$$

$$\begin{array}{r}527\\-319\\\hline\end{array}$$

Adding and Subtracting Money

Add or subtract.

I. What two things can you buy for less than $5.00?

_____

_____

2. How many stuffed elephants can you buy for $10.00?

_____ elephants

How much change will you get?

$ _____

3. How much more does a teddy bear cost than a rubber duck?

$ _____

4. If you had $8.00 to spend, what would you buy?

_____

_____

Adding Equal Groups

Write how many.

1.

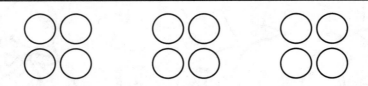

$$\underline{4} + \underline{4} + \underline{4} = \underline{12}$$

2.

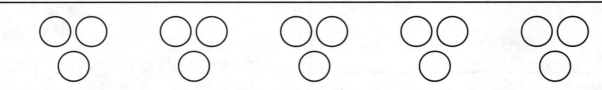

$$\underline{} + \underline{} + \underline{} + \underline{} = \underline{}$$

3.

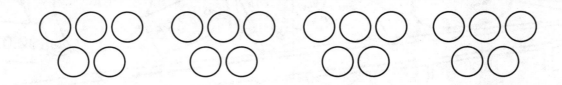

$$\underline{} + \underline{} + \underline{} + \underline{} + \underline{} = \underline{}$$

4.

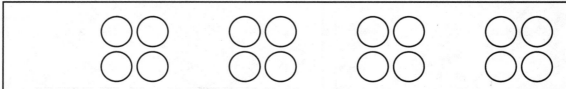

$$\underline{} + \underline{} + \underline{} + \underline{} = \underline{}$$

Multiplying with 2 and 5

Draw and color rows of clown bow ties.

1. 3 rows of 2 red bow ties

How many in all? ___6___

2. 2 rows of 4 green bow ties

How many in all? _____

3. 3 rows of 5 blue bow ties

How many in all? _____

4. 2 rows of 6 yellow bow ties

How many in all? _____

5. 4 rows of 5 orange bow ties

How many in all? _____

6. 5 rows of 6 purple bow ties

How many in all? _____

Multiplying with 3 and 4

Use a number cube.
The first roll will show how many groups.
The second roll will show how many are in each group.
Write the multiplication sentence.
Draw a picture to solve the problem.

1.

_____ × _____ = _____

2.

_____ × _____ = _____

3.

_____ × _____ = _____

4.

_____ × _____ = _____

5.

_____ × _____ = _____

Write Your Problems

Work with a partner.
Fill in the missing numbers in the story.
Draw the picture to solve.

1. Every student gets _____ new pencils. There are _____ new students. How many pencils will they get?

    _____ pencils

2. Miss Keller's room has _____ rows of desks. There are _____ desks in each row. How many desks are in Miss Keller's room? _____ desks

3. There are _____ bikes. There are _____ clowns on each bike. How many clowns are there in all?

    _____ clowns

4. There are _____ wagons. There are _____ children in each. How many children are in the wagons?

    _____ children

How Many in Each Group?

1. How many pieces can you cut that are each 2 units long?

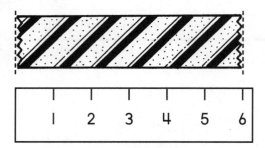

1	2	3	4	5	6

_____

2. How many pieces can you cut that are each 3 units long?

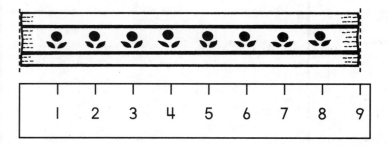

1	2	3	4	5	6	7	8	9

_____

3. How many pieces can you cut that are each 2 units long?

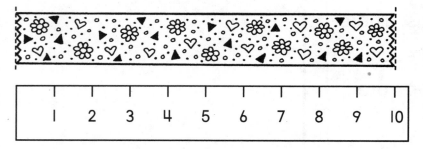

1	2	3	4	5	6	7	8	9	10

_____

4. If you cut 3 pieces of the same length, how long will each piece be?

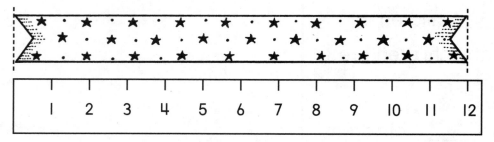

1	2	3	4	5	6	7	8	9	10	11	12

_____ units

How Many Equal Groups?

Draw the groups, using squares.

1. Draw 9 squares in groups of 3.

_____ groups

2. Draw 12 squares in groups of 6.

_____ groups

3. Draw 15 squares in groups of 5.

_____ groups

Problem Solving • Draw a Picture

Look for equal groups in the picture.
Write how many groups, and how many in each.
Write a story problem about the picture.

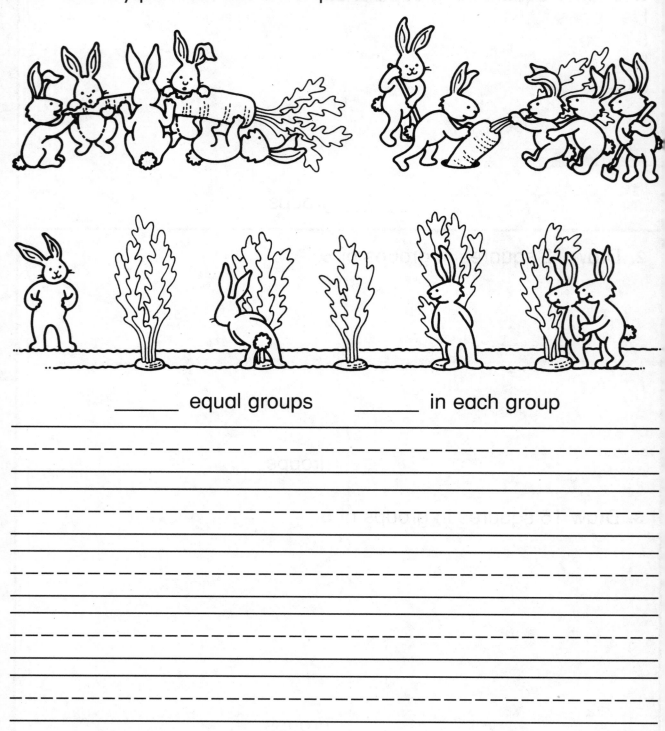

_____ equal groups   _____ in each group

_____
- -
_____
_____
- -
_____
_____
- -
_____
_____
- -
_____
_____
- -
_____

Name _____

Problem Solving • Choose a Strategy

Draw a picture or make a model to solve.

1. Jack buys 25 pieces of gum.
He keeps 5 pieces and gives
5 pieces to each of his friends.
How many friends does Jack
give gum to?

_____ friends

2. Laura has 18 stuffed animals.
She divides them into 2 equal
groups.
How many stuffed animals are
in each group?

_____ stuffed animals

3. Tommy has 2 dogs and
1 cat. He wants to give each
of them 3 treats.
How many treats does he need?

_____ treats

4. Sarah has 30¢.
She has enough to buy 3 new
bows for her hair.
How much does each bow cost?

_____ ¢